TORN PAGE 55/56
9/23 I.D

R0172240863

FamilyFun
Tricks and Treats

By Deanna F. Cook
and the experts at FamilyFun magazine

Disney
EDITIONS

FamilyFun
Tricks and Treats

EDITORS
Deanna F. Cook
and Alexandra Kennedy

MANAGING EDITOR
Priscilla Totten

COPY EDITORS
Paula Noonan, Susan
Roberts, and Laura MacKay

ASSISTANT EDITORS
Nicole Letourneau and
Julia Lynch

CREATIVE DIRECTOR
Hans Teensma,
Impress, Inc.

DESIGNER
Pamela Glaven

ART DIRECTOR
Ginger Barr Heafey

PICTURE EDITOR
Mark Mantegna

ART COORDINATOR
Dana Stiepock

PHOTOGRAPHY
Robert Benson, Michael
Carroll, Jim Gipe, Tom
Hopkins, Ed Judice,
Lightworks Photographic,
Joanne Schmaltz, and
Shaffer/Smith Photography

PRODUCTION
Martha Jenkins and
Jennifer Mayer

**TECHNOLOGY
COORDINATOR**
Luke Jaeger

**CONTRIBUTING
EDITORS**
Jonathan Adolph, Rani M.
Arbo, Ann Hallock, and
Cindy A. Littlefield

This book is dedicated to the readers of *FamilyFun* magazine.

Many of the ideas in this book were adapted from articles in *FamilyFun* magazine. *FamilyFun* is a division of the Walt Disney Publishing Group. To order a subscription, call 800-289-4849.

The staffs of *FamilyFun* and Impress, Inc., conceived and produced *FamilyFun Tricks and Treats* at 244 Main Street, Northampton, MA 01060, in collaboration with Disney Editions, 114 Fifth Avenue, New York, NY 10011.

ISBN 0-7868-6610-1

Printed by Quebecor World, Taunton, MA.

Special thanks to the following *FamilyFun* magazine writers for contributing their spooky Halloween ideas: Lynne Bertrand, Cynthia Caldwell, Laurie Winn Carlson, Tobye Cook, Teresa K. Edmiston, Dorothy Foltz-Gray, Sara B. Heuchling, Vivi Mannuzza, Aline A. Newman, Rebecca Lazear Okrent, Julie Peters, Barbara Rowley, Carolyn Street, Emily B. Todd, and Laura Torres.

We also would like to thank the following stylists: Grace Arias, Suzanne Boucher/Ennis, Melissa Boudreau/Team, Cynthia Caldwell, Catherine Callahan, Erica Ell/Team, Diane Gilbert, Karin Lidbeck, Susan McClelland, Christine Mottaue, Marie Piraino, Edwina Stevenson, Janet Street, Maryellen Sullivan, Stacey Webb, and Lynne Zimmerman.

We also extend our gratitude to *FamilyFun*'s many creative readers who shared with us their ideas for celebrating Halloween. Thanks to Carmen Brown, Sharon and Ian Burch, Nancy Chisholm, Ellen Crumbaker, Kimberly Hardy-Johns, Teresa Hartley, Tracey Hodapp, Dawn and Corey Klonowski, Pam LeBoeuf, Deborah Lee-Quinn, Barbara and Edsel Leix, Tom and Teresa Mason, Amy Mattingly, Viki McCool, Mary Lisa Piseczny, Susan Russo, Debby Seme, Barbara Stockard, Patti Ummel, Susan Wojciechowski, and Susan Yakscoe.

This book would not have been possible without the talented *FamilyFun* magazine staff, who edited and art-directed many of the Halloween articles for the magazine from 1993 to 2000. We also would like to thank our partners at Disney Editions, especially Wendy Lefkon and Rich Thomas.

About the editors:
Deanna F. Cook is the Special Projects Manager of *FamilyFun* magazine and the editor of *FamilyFun's Cookbook*, *FamilyFun's Crafts*, *FamilyFun's Parties*, and *FamilyFun's Cookies for Christmas* from Disney Editions, and the author of *The Kids' Multicultural Cookbook* and *Kids' Pumpkin Projects* from Williamson. She goes trick-or-treating in her Northampton, Massachusetts, neighborhood with her three-year-old daughter, Ella Skye.

Alexandra Kennedy is the Editorial Director of *FamilyFun* and *Disney Magazine*. She and her husband, James, live in Northampton, Massachusetts, with their sons, Jack (a knight for Halloween) and Nicky (a train conductor).

First edition
10 9 8 7 6 5 4 3 2 1

Contents

Clothespin Bat, page 8

4 **Velcome!**

6 **Spooky Crafts and Decorations**

Why go with store-bought when you and your kids can make your own Halloween decorations? Here we feature scarecrows, spiderwebs, and carved pumpkins that will elicit shrieks of delight from every boy and ghoul who comes a-calling.

32 **Wickedly Easy Costumes**

When it comes to creative costumes, you can be the master of disguises. In this chapter, check out dozens of dress-up designs that are quick to assemble, from a Bull-riding Cowboy to a big blue butterfly.

62 **Haunted House Party**

The coolest parents on the block are always the ones who host the Halloween parties. We teach you how to haunt your house, play Eyeball on a Spoon, and craft spooky favors that will make your Halloween party a scream.

76 **Creepy Cuisine**

Halloween calls for a perfectly inelegant menu. And with our easy-to-follow recipes, any kitchen witch can cook up fiendish foods, from Bat Wings to Skeleton Crude-itay.

94 **Index**

Pipe Cleaner Spiders, page 8

Bubble-blowing Ballplayer, page 24

Headless Butler costume, page 42

Velcome!

WHEN DO YOUR kids start talking about Halloween? My daughter begins daydreaming about costumes and trick-or-treating by midsummer, and it's no wonder. This holiday celebrates all the fiendish things kids hold dear — spooky stories and gross-me-out games, sticky candy and plastic spiders, eerie music and the chance to hide their sweet personalities behind makeup and masks.

At *FamilyFun* magazine, Halloween is one of our favorite excuses to get silly. Since October 1992, we've created so many Halloween crafts, costumes, recipes, and party plans, it's frightening. Our readers, parents with kids ages three to 12, have come to depend on our Halloween ideas. Whether they're looking for a costume idea or a creepy snack to bring into their child's classroom, they know they can find it in our October issue.

Good thing. For many parents, myself included, Halloween has gotten trickier over the years. When we were young, the holiday was all about trick-or-treating — we would simply pull together a last-minute costume and spend a few hours collecting candy around the neighborhood. But these days, with Halloween parties and neighborhood costume parades, Halloween has become a monster of a holiday. At each event, we are

looking for more creative ideas — each idea more creative than the last.

But don't be scared. In the pages of this book, you'll find more than a hundred tricks and treats from *FamilyFun* magazine. Each idea has been tested and approved by families like yours and mine. They will be a hit with your kids, just like the duck disguise was with my three-year-old daughter, Ella, who is wearing the costume below.

To find this costume and a host of other homemade ideas, flip through the chapters in this book. Choose a few to try, then let the Halloween celebrations begin … if you dare.

Deanna F. Cook

Ring-Around-a-Ghostie, page 20

CHAPTER ONE

Spooky Crafts & Decorations

HALLOWEEN IS A time of transformation — and not just for humans, who don the masks and face paint, but for the very night itself. The dark seems darker, the moon more ghostly, and even the most friendly front yard, porch, or living room can feel delightfully spooky — especially if you've got a few decorating tricks up your sleeve.

For this chapter, we collected 25 cooler-than-a-crypt decorations from *FamilyFun* magazine. Each craft will elicit shrieks of delight from trick-or-treaters who come a-calling, not to mention cast a spell over your own kids (we've yet to meet a child who can resist making a giant spider or gruesome ghost). But before you get started, brush up on our tips below.

Choose age-appropriate crafts.
The projects in this chapter are for a range in ages. When crafting with a preschooler, choose a project that doesn't require a lot of materials and be prepared to take over when he loses interest. Older kids should be able to handle a larger-scale endeavor (say, the pumpkin-head scarecrow on page 26).

Gather materials before you begin.
For almost all of our crafts, we've used materials that are readily available and inexpensive. But there's nothing worse than getting halfway through a project and realizing you're missing something. Read our materials list carefully and start collecting supplies early (for instance, if

you plan to make Mr. Bottle Bones, on page 14, save your empty milk jugs during the month of October). Also, be sure to stock up on orange and black construction paper, paint, and other basic craft supplies.

Encourage creativity. When making any of our Halloween crafts with your kids, steer toward a finished product, but emphasize the process. The end result, after all, is no more important than the steps that lead up to it. Encourage your kids to customize our crafts (one family we know turned the Ghost Town on page 17 into a replica of their own town, complete with a haunted post office, school, and town hall).

Start a Halloween crafting tradition. Pick a craft you and your family would like to do year after year, such as carving pumpkins or haunting your porch. Over the years, this activity will become a ritual — something you and your kids will look forward to as much as the night of trick-or-treating.

Save your crafts for next Halloween.
Throwing away all your crafts after Halloween may break your child's heart, but saving every last pumpkin paper chain can put you out of house and home. How do you decide what to save? Decorations that are made out of lasting materials, such as Pipe Cleaner Spiders on page 8, can be stored until next Halloween. If the item is too big or won't weather a year in a box, take a photo of it to keep the crafting memory alive.

Ghoulish Masquerade, page 29

Pipe Cleaner Spiders

These fuzzy arachnids are sure to stop your holiday callers in their tracks. For each spider, you'll need 4 pipe cleaners, a 4-hole button, and a pair of stick-on googly eyes. First, bend a pipe cleaner into a V shape. Push the base of the V up through one of the button holes until it protrudes ½ inch. Bend the ½-inch length over the top of the button. Thread the three other pipe cleaners through the remaining buttonholes. Finish the spider by shaping the legs and sticking the googly eyes on the button.

Clothespin Bats

This Halloween, decorate your haunt with a swarm of these easy clip-on paper bats.

MATERIALS
Black, red, and yellow construction paper

Scissors
Glue
Spring-action clothespins

For each bat, cut an extended-wings shape from the black construction paper. Next, cut out an oblong body with pointed ears and feet and glue it onto the wings. Add round, beady eyes cut from yellow or red construction paper. Glue a clothespin to the back of the bat, and it's ready to hang on to a curtain.

A Parade of Pumpkins

Line your windowsill with a row of mini pumpkins. To make one, cut two cups from a cardboard egg carton. Glue the top edge of one cup to the edge of a second cup. Once the glue dries, coat the shell with orange acrylic paint. Let it dry. Poke a hole in the top of the pumpkin using a straightened paper clip. Make a stem and curly vines out of green pipe cleaners or twisted crepe paper and push the ends through the hole. Use a black marker to draw a jack-o'-lantern face.

Jet-black Cats

There's no need to worry about these black paper cats crossing your path. Bright-eyed and bushy-tailed, they're meant to stand on a table or a doorstep as a surprise greeting for Halloween guests.

MATERIALS

- Black poster board
- Scissors
- Pinking shears
- Pencil
- Glue
- Yellow construction paper
- Black marker

To make a cat, cut an 11- by 6-inch rectangle out of the poster board. Fold it in half so that the shorter edges meet and make a crease. Using the crease for the cat's backbone, cut out a four-legged body (see above). Use pinking shears to trim the bottom of each foot to create toes and cut out a bushy, upright tail.

With the regular scissors, make a small vertical snip in the backbone above the hind legs and fit the base of the tail into it.

For the cat's head, use a 6- by 3½-inch rectangle. Match up the short ends and make a sharp crease in the center. Unfold the rectangle and lay it flat so that the short ends are at the top and bottom. Then form ear tabs. With a pencil, mark both sides of the rectangle 2½ inches up from the bottom. Make a diagonal cut from each mark up to the crease (see above). Refold the rectangle and push up the triangular tabs to

create the cat's ears. With the scissors, shape the cat's chin and neck. Then glue on a black poster board nose and whiskers. Add yellow construction paper eyes with black marker pupils. To attach the cat's head to the body, make a cut in the top of the back (above the front legs) and fit the lower edge of the neck into it.

Ghost Prints

This is an instant art project for little ghouls and boys. Have kids fold a piece of black construction paper in half, then dribble white paint into the crease. When they briefly press the paper back together, then open it, a ghost will appear. Add two drops of green paint to make ghostly eyes.

As an alternative to ghost prints, try dribbling black paint onto orange paper to make creepy bats and bugs.

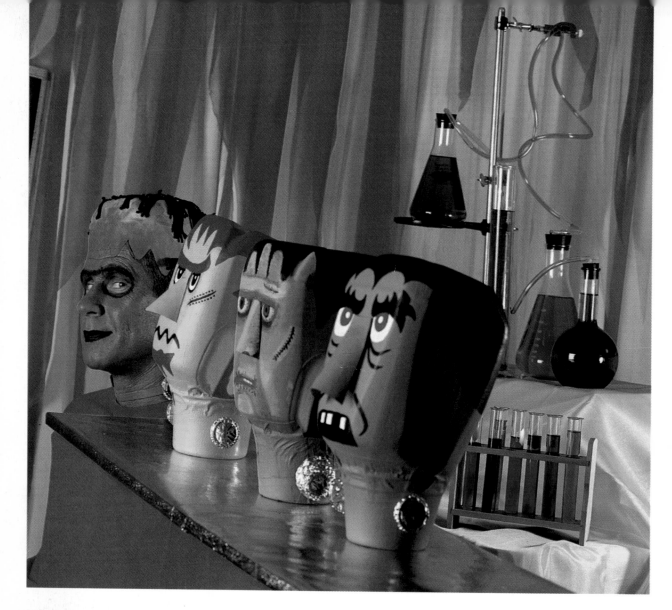

TABLE TOPPER

Monster Jugheads

Ever look at an empty milk jug and think, *Frankenstein*? Well, we did. With a little paint, the dented bottom of a milk jug looks like the monster's extended forehead. These heads look so lifelike, it's hard to tell them from the real thing (as one of these guys is).

MATERIALS

Gallon milk jug
Deli container
Duct tape
Tempera paint
Milk caps
Aluminum foil
Pushpins
Thin piece of cardboard

Turn over the clean milk jug and rest it in the deli container (to make Frankie's thick neck). Attach the jug to the container with the duct tape, then coat it with the tempera paint.

When it's dry, paint bloodshot eyes, scars, and a head of greasy black hair. To create bolts in the sides of the monster's neck, cover milk caps with aluminum foil and attach them with pushpins. A nose can be made out of the cardboard, slipped through a slit cut in the monster's face.

Apple Gals

Don't let their craggy faces fool you. These little old ladies are sweet-natured and make a not-too-spooky decoration for Halloween. And though it takes two weeks for the dolls' heads to dry, the results are worth the wait.

MATERIALS

- **Apple**
- **Paring knife**
- **Colored markers**
- **Wool yarn**
- **Empty 16-ounce plastic bottle**
- **Bottle cork**
- **10- by 16-inch piece of fabric**
- **Rubber band**

When choosing an apple for the doll's head,

the bigger the better — the carved fruit will shrink to about two thirds its original size. Help your child peel and core the apple. Use a knife (parents only) to carve a face on one side. Hollow out deep-set eyes and make a slit for a mouth. For a nose, incise a triangle between the eyes and mouth. Add ears, dimples, and extra facial creases. Store the carved apple in a dry spot until it shrinks. Once the head is dry, your child can use colored markers to enhance the eyes, lips, and cheeks.

To make a wig, cut at least 10 strands of yarn that measure twice the desired hair length plus 2 inches. Bunch the strands together and fold in half. Tie another strand around the yarn 1 inch from the fold to make a loop that can be stuffed into the top of the head.

To make the body, cut the base off the plastic bottle. Plug the top with a cork to serve as the doll's neck. For a dress, wrap the fabric around the bottle so that it extends beyond the top and bottom. Twist a rubber band around the bottle-neck, then fold the cloth down over the band. Finish the doll by pushing the apple onto the cork neck.

Harvest Handstanders

The Crumbakers of Easley, South Carolina, ran into a teeny snafu when assembling these gourd-headed gymnasts — once the 2-by-4 frames were built, mom Ellen was unable to get the pants over them and had to split a leg of each pair and resew it over the frame. For heads, the family went with plastic pumpkin buckets. As a final, spooky touch, each head was illuminated with a Glow Stick on Halloween night.

Witch Crash

Uh, Houston, we have a problem. This witch, whom we first spied on a local tree, should have known better than to get involved in a fly-by-night operation. Still, she's got a few tricks up her sleeve — namely, the ability to provoke hysterics in every trick-or-treater who sees her.

MATERIALS

Black sweatpants
and turtleneck
4 1- by 4-inch boards
Handsaw
Hammer and nails
Black boots
Broom
Rubber dishwashing
gloves
Large drawstring
trash bag
Wig or yarn
Witch's hat

First, choose a crash site for your witch — a tree with a trunk that's sturdy yet not huge in circumference. Ideally, the tree should also be highly visible to passersby.

Measure the sweatpants legs and cut two of the 1 by 4's to a few inches longer than the pants. Slide the wooden "legs" into the sweatpants and, with an assistant's help, nail a leg onto each side of the tree 3 or 4 feet above the ground and parallel to it. For the best illusion, you'll want to have at least a few inches of the legs extending toward the witch's back (so that she appears to have hips). Slide the boots onto the ends of the legs.

Secure the broom in place — roughly parallel to the ground — by nailing it to the tree and one of the wooden legs.

Now cut the other two 1 by 4's to the length of the turtleneck's arms and slip the boards inside the sleeves. Nail an arm to each side of the trunk, parallel to the ground and a few feet above her legs (so that the bottom of the turtleneck just reaches the sweat-pants). Slip the rubber gloves onto the ends of the witch's arms.

Pull the trash bag drawstring tight, then nail the bag in place so it hangs down as a cape. Secure the cape at the bottom as well, so it doesn't blow around.

Nail the wig to the tree, cover it with the hat, then nail the hat in place as well. If you don't have a wig, simply cut a bunch of thick yarn into long strands and tie them together at the top.

Recycled Ghosts

It won't take long to get into the Halloween mood with a few of these packing foam ghosts hanging around your house.

To make some, all you'll need is a pencil, paper, scissors, and a sheet of white packing foam (available at packing or moving supply stores).

First, have your child sketch some simple ghostly figures on paper. Then he can use the ones he likes best as patterns for cutting ghosts from the foam. Be sure to cut out spectral eyes and a mouth.

Post your ghosts in windows using clear tape. Or tie fishing line to the tops of a few ghosts and hang them from tree branches, your front porch, or inside from your ceilings and doorways.

When Halloween is over, pack your ghosts safely away until it's time for them to reappear next season.

Mr. Bottle Bones

Start saving your empty plastic gallon jugs — with a snip here and a hole there, you can resurrect a life-size skeleton.

Punching holes and tying on bones is a job for little kids; cutting out and gluing the pieces together is a job for older children and parents. If you like, you can paint Mr. Bones with glow-in-the-dark paint.

MATERIALS
8 or 9 clean, plastic gallon jugs
Scissors
Craft knife (optional; for parents only)
String
Glue gun (for parents only)
One-hole punch

Head: Choose a jug with a pair of circular indentations opposite the handle and turn it upside down. In the corner, opposite the handle, cut out a large, smiling mouth, centered under the indented "eyes."

Make two small slits in the top of the head and tie a loop of string through them to hang the finished skeleton.

Chest: As shown, cut a vertical slit down the center of a right-side-up jug, directly opposite the handle. Cut and trim away plastic to make the rib cage. Glue the head and chest together at the "neck" by connecting the spouts of the two jugs with a thick band of hot glue. Hold the jugs together for a few minutes until the glue cools.

Shoulders: Cut off two jug handles (leaving a small collar on the ends) and attach them to the chest section with hot glue. Punch a hole at one end of each shoulder.

Hips: Cut all the way around a jug, about 4½ inches up from the bottom. Take the bottom piece and trim away a small rounded half circle from each side to make a four-cornered shape. Punch holes in two opposite corners.

Waist: Cut out two spouts, leaving a ½-inch collar on each. Glue the spouts together and let dry. Then, hot-glue the waist to the bottom of the chest and the top of the hip section.

Arms and legs: Cut eight long bone shapes from the corner sections of three jugs (cut into the curved shape of the jug to make bones even more realistic). From four of these bones, cut out the center to make lower limbs (forearms and shins). Punch a hole through the ends of all eight bones. With string, tie two arm sections to each shoulder, and two leg sections to each hip.

Hands and feet: Let kids trace their hands and feet onto the side of a jug, then cut out the shapes. Punch holes in the hands and feet and tie them to the arms and legs.

Vampire Strikes Back

Holy trash bags,
Batman! This Jurassic-size
bat is a breeze to make —
and breezes are what bring
it to life as well. Suspended
in a tree or from a porch
ceiling, its wings rustle
with all the convincing
creepiness of an Anne Rice
novel.

MATERIALS
- 2 **large black trash
    bags**
- **2-liter plastic soda
    bottle**
- **Black electrical tape**
- **Rubber bands**
- **White plastic lid**
- 2 **red dot stickers**
- 2 **straight sticks**

To make the bat's body,
wrap one of the trash bags
around the plastic bottle
and secure it in place with
the electrical tape.

Create the bat's ears
by pinching two small
bunches of plastic (near
the cap end of the bottle)
and wrapping a rubber

band around the base of
each bunch. Use scissors
to cut a set of fangs out of
the white plastic lid, tape
them in place, then affix
the red stickers for eyes.

Cut open the other
trash bag, lay it flat, then
cut two large bat wings
out of it, roughly in the
shape of the ones shown
above.

Lay one of the wings
flat on the ground and
place one of the sticks just
above it (if necessary, trim

the stick to the wing's
length with clippers). Tape
the three "points" on the
top of the wing to the
stick with electrical tape.
Repeat for the other wing,
then securely tape both
wings to the bat's body.

To hang the bat, simply
nestle the sticks among
the branches of a tree. If
the weather is particularly
windy, you may want to
tape the wings in place, so
your bat won't truly take
flight.

Ghost Town

If your kids just can't wait for Halloween to roll around, let them put all that restless spirit into a tabletop ghost town.

MATERIALS
Paper lunch bags
Cardboard
Newspapers
Markers, crayons, or tempera paint
Assorted materials for landscaping and inhabiting the ghost town

To make a building, trace an unopened paper lunch bag onto a piece of cardboard and then cut out the tracing. Make a second cardboard cutout, then fit the matching cardboard pieces into the bag and stuff the middle with newspaper. Use markers, crayons, or tempera paints to create a store or house (the bottom of the bag will be the roof).

Arrange the buildings on a large piece of cardboard. Then tape down the backs of the bags to the cardboard.

Now you're ready for landscaping. For an autumn tree, fit a branch into a hole cut in the poster board (use glue if necessary). You can use scissors or a craft punch to make miniature tissue-paper leaves. Add a plastic bottle cap basket filled with orange bead "pumpkins" and a stack of miniature dried-grass hay bales.

Haunt your finished village with paper bats, cotton ghosts, and tiny trick-or-treaters. To make a witch, bend a pipe cleaner into an inverted V for a body. Twist a second pipe cleaner around it for arms. Glue on tissue paper boots. For a dress, cut a head hole in a black tissue paper square, then slip it on and tie it with yarn. Glue on thread for hair and a paper hat.

To make a bat, bend a 1-inch length of pipe cleaner into a V, then glue it onto black tissue wings. Use wire to attach the bat to a building or tree.

Make a ghost from white pipe cleaners. Glue cotton batting to the body. Draw on black eyes and a mouth. Tuck the finished ghosts between the buildings. For a trick-or-treater ghost, craft a stick figure from pipe cleaners. Drape a white tissue over the body and then use your fingers to scrunch and shape. Draw on eyes and a mouth.

Ghost Wind Socks

Kids can craft these spooky paper decorations for your porch — and they'll come alive in the breeze.

MATERIALS
   6- by 18-inch piece of white construction paper

Markers or crayons
Crepe paper
Tape
String

For each wind sock, decorate the construction paper with ghostly eyes and a creepy mouth. Roll the paper into a tube and staple the ends together. Cut eight 8-foot-long strips of crepe paper and drape them over the top edge with both ends hanging down to create "tails." Secure with tape. For a handle, cut a 30-inch piece of string and staple the ends to opposite sides of the top of the decoration.

Pumpkin Candleholders

During the month of October, let these festive candleholders light up your dinner table. The flickering light will help set the mood in the days leading up to Halloween. If you can't find mini pumpkins, try using apples instead.

MATERIALS
   Small pumpkins
   Apple corer or small spoon
   Taper candles

To make one candleholder, cut the top off a mini pumpkin, making sure the hole is no bigger than a quarter (parents only). Ask your kids to help remove the seeds from the pumpkin with a small spoon or the tip of an apple corer. Stick the candle into the hole, place on your dinner table, and you're ready for a candlelight dinner.

Dinner Ghosts

Butternut squash, rather than pumpkin, is the Halloween centerpiece at the Hardy-Johns household in Tampa. *FamilyFun* reader Kimberly Hardy-Johns reported that her oldest daughter, Rachael, came up with the idea.

First, Rachael covered three butternut squashes in white paint and let them dry thoroughly. To complete her ghosts, she added a mouth and eyes of black construction paper, using straight pins to attach them. (You could also use a permanent black marker.) As you can see, each squash took on an individual personality.

Ring-Around-a-Ghostie

Why do ghosts never play tricks on Halloween? Because everyone can see right through them! It's perfectly all right, however, if they play with each other, as this spectral sextet demonstrates. Let your kids give each one a happy — or scary — face.

MATERIALS
- 6 **dowels**
- 6 **small white trash bags**
- **Newspaper**
- **Masking tape**
- 6 **white sheets**
- **String**
- **Black permanent markers**

First, find a good location for your gathering of ghosts. They look especially good when circling a central pole, such as a tree or lamppost.

Next, cut your dowels to the height you'd like your ghosts to be (the ghosts shown above are 4 feet high). Remember: the larger the ghosts, the more sheets you'll need to use.

To make a ghost head, stuff a trash bag with crumpled newspaper or leaves to the size you like. Push one of the dowels into the bag, then wrap masking tape around the neck to secure.

Drape a sheet over each head and tie a piece of string around each neck. You may need to experiment with cutting your sheets to the right size; here we used a queen-size sheet for each ghost and rounded the bottom edges to the desired length.

Draw a face on each ghost using markers.

Gather your ghosts around the tree or pole with a foot or two between each one. Push the dowels into the earth so that the sheets touch the ground. Angle the ghosts so that they are leaning slightly backward, then knot the corners of the sheets together as if the ghosts were holding hands.

PUMPKINS

Wicked Witch of the Midwest

With help from their grandson, Joey, *FamilyFun* readers Barbara and Edsel Leix of Byron, Michigan, conjured up this green-faced witch to haunt their front yard.

MATERIALS

Pumpkin
Green spray paint
Tempera paint
2 marbles
Black wig or yarn
Small nails and
　hammer
Witch's hat and
　cape

First, coat a pumpkin with the spray paint. Once it has dried, use the tempera paint to add features, such as a gaping mouth and white eyes (here we carved deep-set eyes, painted them white, then inserted marble "eyeballs"). For a nose, use the stem; for hair, use a wig or yarn. Secure the nose and hair to the pumpkin by hammering small nails through them. Top off your witch with a cape and a big black witch's hat.

FamilyFun **Tricks and Treats**

Say Boo!

What can you and your kids do with four odd-size pumpkins? This solution — making each a letter in a Halloween message — is so clever it's scary.

MATERIALS
4 **small pumpkins**
Marker
Paring knife or carving tool
Large spoon
4 **candles**

First, draw the letters and exclamation point on the pumpkins with a marker. Cut the tops off with a sharp knife (parents only). Cut a small hole in each cap to allow heat from the candle to escape. Remove seeds and scrape the walls until they are about 1 inch thick. Cut out the letters with a knife or pumpkin-carving tool. Light a candle in each one.

LAWN DECORATION
Trash Bag Tarantula

As Charlotte might say, this is Some Spider. Her long legs are made from trash bags, as is her over-stuffed body. Perch her on a pile of leaves in your front yard and see which trick-or-treaters are daring enough to tiptoe past her wicked web.

MATERIALS
18 **large black trash bags**
Leaves or newspaper
Black electrical tape
3 **large red plastic party cups**
Clothesline (optional)

To make the spider's body, stuff one trash bag full of dry leaves or crumpled newspaper. Tie the bag closed, then flip it upside down. For the head, stuff a second bag (not as full as the first), tie it closed, and tape it to the body.

To make one of the legs, roll up two trash bags together lengthwise and wrap them with electrical tape at both ends and at two points along the leg to make joints. Roll up seven more legs, then cut four small slits in each side of the spider's body and slip the legs in place.

Cut the white lip off two of the red plastic cups, then tape them onto the spider's body to make her beady red eyes. For the fangs, cut two triangles out of the third plastic cup (or another piece of white plastic) and tape them onto the spider so that the white side faces up.

Perch your spider atop a big pile of dry leaves. If you'd like to create a web for her, simply weave and tie lengths of clothesline or twine across your porch. If you want to give your spider an extra-scary effect, you might also tie a few unlucky stuffed animals to her web.

Wicked Webs

For a spidery nighttime display on Halloween, *FamilyFun* reader Susan Yakscoe of Sterling, Virginia, had her class of preschoolers and her son's third grade class make glow-in-the-dark marble-art spiderwebs.

To make one, cut circles from black construction paper so that they just fit inside disposable cake pans. Drop marbles into small cups of white tempera paint. Use a spoon to take the marbles out of the paint and drop them into the cake pan. Rock the pans back and forth and from side to side. Dip the marbles a second time to make a more intricate web.

While the paint is still wet, sprinkle glow-in-the-dark glitter on the web. After the paint dries, put spider stickers on your web and head for a dark room to see your creations glow.

Turnip the Lights

Carving jack-o'-lanterns began in ancient Ireland, where kids used hollowed-out turnips to light the way on a dark Halloween night. Use a turnip to make this nonflammable, yet spooky, trick-or-treat lantern.

MATERIALS
- **Turnip**
- **Paring knife**
- **Spoon**
- **Flashlight**

Slice off the very top of the turnip and hollow out the inside using a sharp paring knife and a spoon (parents only). Then carefully carve facial features in one side. Cut a circle in the bottom of the turnip to fit over the end of the flashlight. Finally, turn on the flashlight to give Jack a glow.

Bubble-blowing Ballplayer

The Klonowskis, *FamilyFun* readers from Bourbonnais, Illinois, turned their pumpkin into a gum-chewing ballplayer. For eyes, they carved holes in the hollowed-out shell and tacked white paper behind them. Then they used acrylic paints and colored markers to add eye black below the eyes. For the gum bubble, they blew up a small pink balloon and pulled the knotted end through a small hole in the pumpkin's shell. As a finishing touch, they put on a baseball cap.

Unidentified Flying Pumpkin

When it came to celebrating Halloween, *FamilyFun* reader Ian Burch, age nine, of Sanbornton, New Hampshire, took the concept to its outer limits with this galaxy-cruising pumpkin. His mom, Sharon, lent a hand spraying the hollowed-out pumpkin with silver paint while Ian painted and decorated a cardboard ramp complete with descending aliens (gumball machine treasures affixed with hot glue). Ian even brought his creation to school for the annual pumpkin contest, where it won first place for Most Original.

PUMPKINS

Paint a Pumpkin

You'd have to be a ghoul not to love carving pumpkins, but knives can sometimes be a little too scary. These no-cut jack-o'-lanterns can be made by even the littlest kids — and they won't rot before the big night.

MATERIALS
Pumpkins
Newspaper
Tempera or acrylic
  paint
Plastic yogurt
  containers filled
  with water

First, choose clean, dry pumpkins that show no signs of rotting. Then cover your work surface with newspaper (tape it down with masking tape so it doesn't slip off).

Set out the pumpkins, paints, paintbrushes, and plastic yogurt containers filled with water (for rinsing the brushes). Let the kids paint goofy, surprised, or creepy faces on the pumpkins. (Note: For painted features that won't wash away in the rain, use acrylic instead of tempera paint.)

Meet Mr. Pumpkinhead!

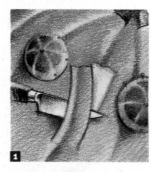

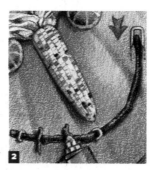

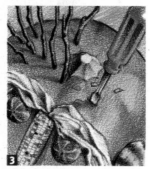

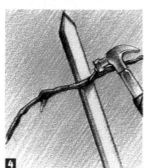

Even if this pumpkin-head scarecrow fails to scare off the birds, so what? Your family will have a lot of laughs putting him together — and he'll certainly attract some notice from your neighbors.

MATERIALS

  2 **small gourds**
     Straight pins
  1 **large pumpkin**
  1 **large oval gourd**
     Hot glue gun
  1 **ear Indian corn**
     Florist U-pins
     Sticks for mouth
       and hair
     Screwdriver
  1 **36-inch-long**
       branch for arms
     Hammer and nails
     2- by 3-inch by 6-
       foot wood stake
       with pointed
       ends
     Scary old clothes

1 Slice the small gourds in half; you will use their bottoms for eyes. Attach them by pushing straight pins through the outer edges of the gourds and into the pumpkin. Angle the pins inward for a stronger bond. Cut the large gourd in half to make ears; attach them in the same manner.

Cut away some of the outer skin where the nose will go, as shown. Wipe away excess moisture with a towel. (The nose will stick better this way.)

2 With a glue gun (a parent should do this), attach an ear of corn on top of the cut area. Place the corn so that the husks fall over the eyes like eyebrows. Attach an arched stick with U-pins to form a mouth. Glue 1-inch sticks across the mouth to create a toothy grin.

3 For the scarecrow's spiked hair, use a screwdriver to poke holes in his head about 2 inches apart around the top, back, and sides of the pumpkin. Push 4- to 8-inch sticks into the holes until secure.

4 Nail a branch centered on the wooden stake where the arms should be. (Leave plenty of room for the head to be placed on top of the stake.)

Now you're ready to dress the scarecrow in old clothes. Ours looks quite sporting in the style that used to be called traditional but is now called grunge. Push the stake about 1 foot into the ground and support with rocks.

Hold the pumpkin head over the top and push it down onto the stake until the point reaches the top of the pumpkin. Now, step back and watch the crows scatter.

FUN FACT

The Story of Scarecrows

Once upon a time, farmers hired kids with slingshots to guard their fields. Many Native Americans, who had a more cooperative relationship with nature, placed live sentries in their fields to wave their arms, yell, and generally carry on. But the day came when people found more rewarding things to do. Thus was born the scarecrow.

It seemed like a great idea. But birds — despite the opinion we hold about their brains — figure out rather quickly that though scarecrows look threatening, they don't attack and eat birds very often. A scarecrow's usefulness in warding off flocks works for about a week — or until one bird fuels up and departs without a ruffled feather.

Ghostly Graveyard

Complete with restless spirits and headstones, this mini cemetery is big on Halloween spirit. Here's how you and your kids can conjure up one.

MATERIALS

- Cardboard box
- White glue
- Tissue paper
- Tree branches
- Leaf hole punch
- Corrugated cardboard
- Materials for Gauze Ghosts (page 29)
- Toothpicks
- Markers
- 3 plastic berry boxes
- Pipe cleaners

Graveyard: For the graveyard base, use a shallow box. Mix the glue with a bit of water, brush the solution onto the bottom and sides of the box, and press on green tissue paper.

Gnarly Trees: Trim dead branches into trees using garden clippers. To anchor them in the graveyard, cut holes in the box bottom and wedge in the branch bases. Then use a miniature leaf-shaped paper punch to make tissue paper leaves; glue onto the limbs.

Scared-stiff Ghosts: Follow the Gauze Ghosts directions at right, but make them mini.

Mossy Tombstones: Cut headstone shapes from corrugated cardboard, brush on diluted white glue, and then wrap them in black, brown, or red tissue paper. Apply another coat of glue and cover with white tissue paper. Once the glue has dried, use markers to print on names. Finally, insert one end of a toothpick into the bottom of each stone and push the other end through the box bottom.

Wrought-Iron Fence: Cut the side panels from three plastic berry boxes. Arrange the panels (with the basket rims down) into a rectangular yard, using snippets of pipe cleaner to link them together. Use one of the berry box bottoms for a gate. Set the assembled fence on the box bottom, then push pipe cleaner posts down through the links and into the tissue-covered cardboard to hold it in place.

Gauze Ghosts

It takes practically nothing to make this family of mischievous sprites.

MATERIALS

> Plastic milk jugs or juice bottles
> Aluminum foil
> White gauze or cheesecloth
> Liquid laundry starch

Collect an assortment of different-size milk jugs or juice bottles. Top each one with a ball of crumpled foil.

Next, cut white gauze or cheesecloth into 18-inch squares (one square per ghost). Dip the gauze into a bowl filled with laundry starch. Pull the squares out one at a time and squeeze out the excess moisture. Drape a square over each bottle.

To shape the shoulders and arms, loosely pile crumpled foil near the bottle and drape the gauze over it. Flare out the lower edges of the gauze and let dry overnight. (To make the mini ghosts on page 28 or the dog at left, drape a small gauze square over shaped foil.) Once dry, lift the ghosts from their bottles, and they'll stand freely.

Ghoulish Masquerade

It was a white pumpkin that inspired the Mason family, *FamilyFun* readers from Aurora, Colorado, to create this clever camouflage job. When Dad (Tom Mason) spotted this unusual variety, he was motivated to create a ghost masquerading as a pumpkin. Tom says that he wanted "something a little surreal but nonthreatening and fun" to fit in with the Masons' high-concept Halloween decorating theme of masks on masks. (Other creations included Frankenstein's monster wearing eyeball glasses and Darth Vader sporting a fake nose.) Using acrylic paints, he simply painted the face orange and added white, black, and yellow features. Are you unable to find a white pumpkin in your area? You can fake it by painting an orange pumpkin white, leaving only the face area orange.

Jack-o'-lanterns

It's the witching hour again: time to carve the most eye-popping jack-o'-lantern in the neighborhood. Here are some tips for a glowing pumpkin.

MATERIALS

> Pumpkin
> Water-based marker
> Paring and chef
>   knives
> Large spoon
> Potato peeler or
>   X-Acto knife
> Short votive candle

First, select a pumpkin. Look for a large, heavy, evenly shaped pumpkin. If it will be lit by votive candles, it should be at least 9 inches high. Clean and dry your pumpkin.

Next, consider the face you want to carve. A pumpkin may suggest a particular face by its strange shape or lumps, or even a curly stem. Draw your design on paper, then copy it onto the pumpkin with a water-based marker (wipe any mistakes with a wet paper towel).

To get the top off, draw a circle an even distance around the stem and begin cutting with a large knife (parents only). To prevent the lid from slipping inside, cut at an angle so the outside of the lid is bigger than the inside.

Scoop out the seeds and stringy flesh with a large spoon and set aside for roasting (see recipe on page 83). Scrape the inside until it's smooth.

When you carve your face, work from the center out; create the eyes before the eyebrows and save the mouth for last. Gently push the cutouts either into or out of the pumpkin.

You can further define your jack's expressions, but the finer carving calls for an X-Acto knife, and small curves are easier to do with the end of a potato peeler. Cut around a shape at an angle, not deeply (⅛ inch is enough). Peel away the strip and expose the inner flesh.

Make holes large enough to provide air for the candle flame. Flatten a spot in the base of the pumpkin for the votive candle and place it inside the pumpkin. Light it, place the lid on top, and turn out the lights — and remember to blow out the candle before you go to bed.

Creative Designs

The Scream (above): Have your child hold a pumpkin like a basketball. Trace her hands, then cut out the shapes. Finally, carve a simple face.

Stack-o'-lantern (opposite): Choose three pumpkins: a big one for the bottom with progressively smaller ones above. Cut the tops off all three, trimming until the stack fits. Carve each, light with candles, and restack.

Jack-in-a-Jack (left): You'll need two pumpkins: a large one and one small enough to fit inside it. Carve both pumpkins. Place a votive candle inside the small pumpkin, then place inside the big pumpkin, and put on the lids.

Pumpkin-carving Safety

Use your judgment about whether your child can handle a knife safely. Some basic safety rules pertain: always carve with an adult, never cut toward yourself, and grip the handle firmly. Do not work with a dull knife. As a safer alternative, use the pumpkin-carving tools from craft and discount stores.

CHAPTER TWO

Wickedly Easy Costumes

HAVE YOU EVER stayed home on trick-or-treat duty and wondered, as hordes of fantastically clad kids stepped up to your door, *How did they ever come up with that?* That sense of amazement is what we at *FamilyFun* magazine feel every October as we open letter after letter bearing outstanding costume ideas from our readers.

Over the years, we've discovered that conceiving a terrific costume doesn't have to be tricky. With some materials from a fabric or craft store and a little creativity, any parent-child team can pull one off. And though it does take some time, the payoff is great: a homemade costume stands out in a neighborhood — and in our memories — more than its factory-made cousin.

So if you're stumped for a costume idea this year, take a look at what many clever families — and the craft experts at *FamilyFun* magazine — have designed. All of the costumes are easy to make, cost less than $40, and can withstand the rigors of a night out. When you're ready to begin, just follow our step-by-step directions and the tips below, and your family will be dressed to thrill this Halloween.

Start with a great idea. The best costumes come from a child's imagination — after all, Halloween is a chance for kids to act out a fantasy. To help your child pick his disguise, have him brainstorm a list of all his favorite things, be it a food, an animal, or a toy (this works

every year for *FamilyFun* reader Teresa Hartley of Richmond, Virginia, whose son Bryan created the popular LEGO costume on page 54). Once you've settled on an idea, look for it in this chapter or adapt it from one of our designs.

Stock up on supplies. Start collecting materials to make the costume at least two weeks before Halloween. You might need to head to a fabric store (for fabric, felt, and a glue gun) and a craft store (for fabric paints, craft foam, and face paints). Also, to keep costs down, you can hit a thrift shop for cheap hats, glasses, and other accessories, or a discount store for on-sale leggings, turtlenecks, and sweat suits. Don't forget to look for recycled boxes and other items around the house too.

Be creative and flexible. When crafting a costume, encourage your child to add his own touches. Choose a favorite color, add an accessory, or personalize the costume with paint. If given plenty of room for imagination, your child will take tremendous pride in making his costume.

Keep safety in mind. Be sure your homemade costume is sturdy and fits well (you don't want your child to trip or knock over any poorly placed jack-o'-lanterns). If he's wearing a mask, be sure it doesn't obscure his vision. And all kids should carry a flashlight and wear reflective tape.

Don't forget to take a photo. Be sure to preserve your child's creativity by taking a photograph just before he heads out the door. Keep the memories in a special Halloween album.

Heavenly Angel, page 39

Butterfly Blue

This dainty butterfly costume is sure to attract compliments. Also, with its hat, boots, and plump belly, it's just right for those cool autumn nights when most exquisite creatures prefer to stay safely tucked into their cocoons. If you wish, tailor the color scheme to your child's preference (or to wardrobe items you may already have on hand).

MATERIALS

- 2 **sheets of corrugated cardboard**
- **Utility knife**
- **Tempera paints**
- **Cellophane**
- 8 **feet of cording**
- 2 **googly eyes**
- 2 **Silly Straws**
- **Knit ski cap**
- **Blue shirt, tights, and socks**
- **Sneakers**
- **48-inch piece of fiberfill batting**
- **24-inch piece of nylon rope**
- **Diaper pins**

The wings: 1 Draw the butterfly wings on one piece of the cardboard that extends roughly from the top of your child's hips to the back of his head and no more than 8 inches beyond his shoulders (our butterfly has a wingspan of about 2 feet). Draw a simple decorative pattern on the wings. Cut out the wing shape and pattern using a utility knife (parents only). Trace the shape onto the second piece of cardboard and cut out. Paint one side of each wing shape. When dry, place one wing, paint side down, on your work surface and cut pieces of cellophane to lay over the cutouts in the wing. Glue the second wing on top so that the cellophane is sandwiched in place. As shown, poke three holes in the wing and thread the cording through them so it hangs evenly.

The antennae: 2 Glue one googly eye to the tip of each Silly Straw, then tape the straws, as shown, about halfway down the ski hat. Fold up the brim to hide the tape.

The body: 3 Have your child put on the shirt, tights, and sneakers. Pull the socks on over his sneakers. Wrap the batting around his middle a few times, then tightly wrap the piece of nylon over the batting. Use a few diaper pins (for safety's sake) to pin the nylon in place.

Assembly: Your child should put one arm through each cord strap, so he wears the wings like a backpack. Run the cord ends around his waist a few times and tie in place.

Roly-Poly Skunk

When it comes to costumes, *FamilyFun* reader Mary Lisa Piseczny of Colonie, New York, employs two rules: her children have to be warm, and they have to look great. So, Mom made this charming, bushy-tailed skunk from a cozy black sweat suit and faux fur.

MATERIALS

> White and black faux fur
> White and black thread
> Black hooded sweatshirt and sweatpants
> Foam packing peanuts
> Nylon thread
> Black sneakers
> Black face paint

The body: **1** Cut a large oval of white faux fur and sew it on the front of the sweatshirt. Cut a long strip of white faux fur. Starting at the top front of the hood, sew a stripe down the back of the hood to the bottom of the sweatshirt (the photo shows how the shirt and tail should align).

The ears: To make an ear, cut two ear shapes from the black faux fur

and sew them together. Repeat for the other ear, then sew both ears to the hood on each side of the white stripe. Trim the fur on the ears if it's too fluffy.

The tail: **2** Cut a rectangle with a rounded end from the black faux fur and a matching one from the white. Sew the two together, leaving the flat ends open. Stuff with packing peanuts, then sew the ends shut. Sew the flat end of the tail to the bottom rear of the sweatshirt. To make the tail stand up, sew nylon thread through the top of the tail and attach it to the back of the sweatshirt.

Assembly: Have your child put on the sweatpants, sweatshirt, and black sneakers. Finally, add face paint whiskers.

VARIATIONS
Farm Friends

With a new color scheme and rearranged fur, the skunk costume is easily adapted.

Dog: Use spotted fur, a thinner tail, floppy ears, and face paint nose and whiskers.

Squirrel: Use a brown sweat suit and faux fur.

Pig: Use a pink sweat suit, a store-bought nose, and pink craft foam ears.

Sheep: Try a white sweat suit adorned with cotton balls and a tinkling bell collar.

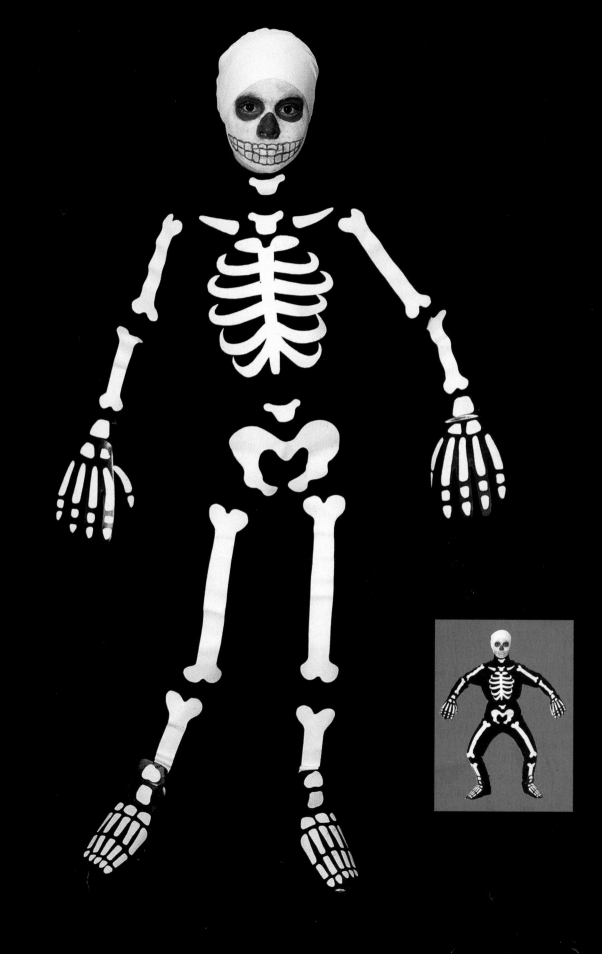

Heavenly Angel

An angel on Halloween? Such a costume may seem incongruous on this mischievous holiday, but somebody has to keep an eye on all the little devils running around.

MATERIALS

Corrugated cardboard
Gold spray paint
White fabric or sheet (approximately 2 yards long by 1 yard wide)
2 yards of gold ribbon (optional)
8-foot length of gold cording
5-foot strand of star garland (available at party stores)

The wings: **1** Draw a fanciful wing shape on the piece of cardboard. It should extend roughly from the top of your child's hips to the back of her head and no more than 8 inches beyond her shoulders (our angel has a 2-foot wingspan). Cut out the shape. Poke three holes — two near the top, one near the bottom, as shown — in the wings. In a ventilated area, spray-paint the wings gold.

The robe: **2** Fold the piece of fabric in half so the two short ends meet. In the center of the fold, cut a slit for your child's head. Slip the robe over her head and have her stand with arms extended. If the robe is too long, cut or hem it; if you wish, attach a stripe of gold ribbon with a loose running stitch about 6 inches up from the bottom hem.

Assembly: Thread one end of the gold cord through one of the top wing holes and the other cord end through the other top hole. Adjust so the ends hang evenly. Hold the wings up to your child's back, laying one cord over each shoulder. Cross the cords over her chest, then around to her back and through the bottom hole in the wings. Wrap the cord ends under the base of the wings and then belt them around her waist. For the halo, wind the star garland into a hoop shape.

Kitty Cat

This kitty costume is the cat's meow. Made from a turtleneck and furry fleece, it will keep your child purring with delight even on a brisk night. The fleece and fusible web are available at fabric stores.

MATERIALS

Black craft foam
Stapler
Rust, gray, and black fleece
Wide headband
Hot glue gun
2 yards fusible web
Ivory turtleneck, leggings, and gloves
½-inch-wide elastic band
Needle and thread (optional)
Wire hanger
Pliers
Child's belt
1 ivory tight leg or knee-high sock
Fiberfill batting
2 white pipe cleaners
Self-adhesive Velcro dots

Head: ◼ First, cut two wide triangles out of the black craft foam for the ears. To give the ears shape, fold each one in half and staple it once along the fold. Next, cut a triangular piece of rust fleece to fit over the top of the headband and extend over your child's forehead (for a calico effect, we glued a black fleece scrap under the rust). Cut rounded notches for the ears on either side, as shown. Hot-glue the underside of the fabric to the headband, then hot-glue the ears onto the fur.

Shirt, leggings, and gloves: Cut a variety of spots from the different colors of fleece. Cut a matching piece of fusible web for each spot. Fuse the web to the underside of your spots with a warm iron, according to package directions. Arrange the spots over the shirt, leggings, and gloves. Then remove the paper backing and iron on one spot at a time. (Because fleece is so plush, you may find it easier to iron from the inside of the clothing.)

Shoes: ◼ From contrasting colors of fleece, cut out a pair of oval shapes with straight tops (basically, a U shape, big enough to cover your child's shoe). Cut a length of elastic to fit around your child's shoe. Fold the flat edge of the fur over the elastic and staple or stitch it in place. Staple or stitch the elastic band into a loop.

Tail: ◼ Use pliers to bend the wire hanger into a long loop for the tail.

Bend a small circle at the top for attaching the belt. Pull the belt through the circle so the tail hangs from the middle of the belt. Lightly stuff the toe of the tight leg or knee-high with batting, then slip it over the wire tail. Finish stuffing the stocking with the batting. Pull the open end around the wire circle and sew or hot-glue it in place. Cut spots and stripes out of the fleece, then stitch or glue them onto the tail.

Whiskers: Twist two white pipe cleaners together in the middle. Cut a length of elastic band to fit around your child's face, then tie the center of the band to the pipe cleaner twist. Knot the ends of the band together.

Assembly: Have your child put on the calico leggings, turtleneck, and gloves. Buckle the tail belt around her waist. Slip the furry feet over her shoes (to help hold the fabric in place, attach one side of a Velcro dot to the underside of the fur and the other side to the toe of the shoe).

The Boxers

If your child really wants to look like a knockout this Halloween, here's the perfect getup.

MATERIALS
1 **pair of red adult sport socks**
Fiberfill batting
Needle and thread or 2 safety pins
Black yarn
1 **sheet poster board**
Child's belt
Corrugated cardboard
Aluminum foil
Duct tape
Black marker
Athletic shorts
Sport socks
Sneakers
Bathrobe
Athletic tape
Black face paint stick (optional)

The gloves: 1 Form the socks into the shape of boxing gloves, using the heel of the sock for the thumb and the toe of the sock for the fingers, as shown. Stuff with batting, then tuck the ends of the socks inside the gloves to cover the batting and form a cuff. Sew or pin the thumb to the hand, as shown. Next, attach the gloves to enough black yarn to drape over the child's shoulders.

The belt: 2 From the poster board, cut a rectangle with rounded ends that fits most of the way around your child's waist (the ones here are 5 by 17 inches). Cut a vertical slit on either side and slide his belt through (he'll wear the buckle in the back). If

you wish, color the poster board brown. Cut a 6-inch circle out of the corrugated cardboard, wrap with aluminum foil, and secure the back with duct tape. Write "Champ" on the front of the circle with black marker. Duct-tape the circle to the poster board belt.

Assembly: Have your child put on the shorts, socks, sneakers, robe, and champ belt. Drape the gloves around his shoulders, then wrap athletic tape around his hands. Finally, use the face paint stick to draw a black eye.

TRICK COSTUME

Headless Butler

To dress up like this ghoulish giant, first make a large cardboard tube out of poster board and tape (it should be about 1½ feet high). Cut two curves in the bottom so it rests comfortably on your child's shoulders. Measure and cut a hole in the tube for your child to put his head through. Cover the top of the tube with red fabric and dress it up with a shirt and jacket. With your child's face poking through the shirt, and with the sleeves tied under his chin, it will look as if this butler is carrying his own head.

MY GREAT IDEA

Soccer Star

This sporty costume idea from Susan Wojciechowski of New Baltimore, Michigan, was a real kick for her son Matt, eight, to wear on Halloween. To make the costume, she followed the directions for the pumpkin suit on page 61, but instead of using orange felt, she used white felt. She then cut pentagons out of black felt and sewed them on the soccer ball. She glued some onto a baseball cap, too. Matt wore a black turtleneck and sweatpants under his all-star soccer ball.

Bull-riding Cowboy

This ingenious cowpoke costume comes from reader Viki McCool of Bryan, Texas. A pair of suspenders holds the bull in place, leaving our hero free to tip his hat to collect goodies.

MATERIALS

Large topless
cardboard box
Sheet of cardboard
Acrylic paints
White leggings
Small cardboard
box
Egg carton cups
Glue
Wire coat hanger
Denim shorts
Button-down shirt
Jeans and belt
Clip suspenders
Newspaper
Cowboy accessories

The bull: **1** Cut a child-size hole in the bottom of the large box. From the cardboard sheet, cut out cowboy boots and the bull's ears, horns, back legs, and tail. With paint, add brown and white spots to the box, back legs, and tail as well as the leggings. Decorate the ears, boots, and horns as shown. Glue the tail and back legs onto the box.

The head: Cut two nostril holes and two eye sockets in the smaller box, insert the egg carton cups, and glue in place. Draw irises in the eyes and paint the head. Cut two slits on both sides of the head and insert the horns and ears. For the neck, twist a wire coat hanger into a spring. Poke one end of the hanger through the back of the smaller box and tape. Poke the other end through the front of the large box near the top and tape.

Assembly: **2** Have your child wear the spotted leggings, denim shorts, and button-down shirt. Run a belt through the front loops of the jeans and the back of the shorts and fasten, as shown. Once he's standing in the bull, lay the suspenders over his shoulders, then clip them to the front and back opening of the box. Stuff the jeans with newspaper and insert the cowboy boots. Accessorize with a rope, bandanna, cowboy hat, and gloves.

Piece of Pizza

Cheesy and fun, this pizza costume comes with all the toppings. It's an easy, low-budget design, created by *FamilyFun* reader Carmen Brown from Findlay, Ohio, for her three-and-a-half-year-old daughter, Miranda.

MATERIALS

- 2-foot-wide piece of ½-inch-thick foam twice your child's height (available at fabric stores)
- 6 large paper fasteners
- Clothespins
- Hot glue gun
- Red and yellow spray paint
- 2 sponges
- Acrylic paint
- Felt
- Pizza box
- Red shoelaces
- White sweatshirt, tights, and shoes

The slice: **1** To make the crust, fold over about 10 inches of foam at one of the narrow ends and attach it with evenly spaced paper fasteners. **2** Fold the entire sheet of foam in half lengthwise. With a marker, draw a wide triangle rising from the crust to the top of the foam, as shown. Cut out the triangle shape through both pieces, using clothespins to connect the sheets. Apply a line of hot glue, about 6 inches at a time, approximately 1 inch from the outside edge. Press the layers together firmly for a few seconds after gluing. When dry, slip the pizza over your child's head and mark where her forehead and chin are on the front and where her shoulders are on the back. Cut out a circle for her face in the front layer. **3** Cut two circles for her arms in the back layer.

The toppings: In a ventilated area, spray-paint the front of the pizza red and the back and crust yellow. When dry, sponge-paint on white cheese and brown grill marks. Cut out felt toppings and attach with hot glue. For the candy bag, tape closed a clean pizza box, cut out one flap, and tie on red shoelace handles.

Assembly: Have your child put on the white sweatshirt, tights, and shoes. Then help her slip on the slice with her head and arms poking through.

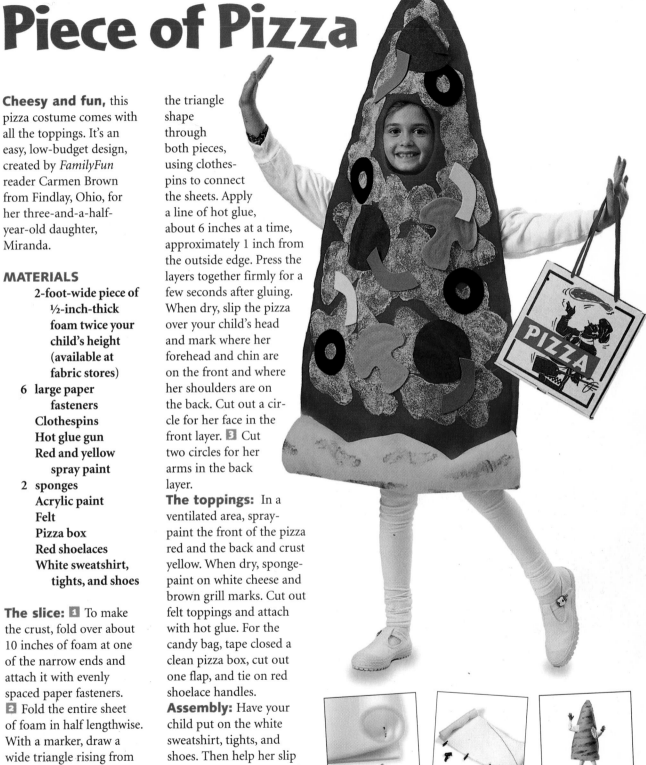

Frankenstein

It's no small feat to fill Frankenstein's shoes — unless, of course, you start by dismembering your own sneakers. From wiggling green toes to a jughead skull, this costume will please the pickiest mad doctor.

MATERIALS

Plastic gallon jug
Green acrylic paint
Nail
Silver pipe cleaners
Masking tape
2 ⅝-inch bolt/washer/ nut combinations
1 yard black plush fur
Mounting tape
Black elastic cord
Old blue jeans
Old canvas sneakers
Black T-shirt
Green blazer
Green plastic gloves (available at hardware stores)
Green socks
Cotton batting
Green face paint

The head: **1** To create Frank's square head, cut the spout and handle off the plastic jug. Paint the front and sides green. Once dry, add silver pipe cleaner stitches to his forehead. To do this, use a nail to poke holes in the jug, then thread the pipe cleaners through the holes so they resemble stitches. Fold the pipe cleaner ends flat on the inside and cover with masking tape so they won't scratch your child's head. **2** Next, add the bolts to the sides of Frank's head. Poke large holes at the temples with the point of a pair of scissors. Thread the bolt from the inside of the head to the outside, then slide on the washer and screw on the nut. Cut Frank's hairpiece out of plush fur in the shape shown. Attach to the front, sides, and back of the jug head with mounting tape. Poke two small holes at the bottom of the headpiece and thread the elastic cord through for a chin strap.

Pants and shoes: **3** Cut the cuffs off the old jeans, then make foot-long fringes up the pant legs. To doctor the sneakers, unlace them and cut off the tongues and the toes, leaving the soles and sides intact, as shown.

Relace the sneakers.

Assembly: Put on the T-shirt, jeans, blazer, jug headpiece, and rubber gloves. Next, put on the green socks and stuff the toes with cotton batting. Lace up the sneakers, apply face paint, and you're child will be ready to fill the big guy's shoes.

FACE PAINT

Bug Attack

Kids will bug out with this creepy face paint design. Use an insect guide for reference if you wish, but don't worry about making the bug shapes exact. Instead, concentrate on making them three-dimensional by painting them on in layers.

With a beige shade (mix orange, blue, and red paint), paint a shadow for each bug, a little bigger than the insect you plan to paint on top. (For extra creepiness, add bug bite marks near some of the shadows.) Next, paint on the bugs, leaving a margin of the beige undercoat visible along the edges. Top each bug with a dab of white face paint (to give them shiny shells). For a final touch, spray on temporary silver hair color and bobby-pin on assorted plastic bugs.

Movie Stars

Fashion trends may come and go, but as any movie star knows, true glamour is never out of style. The centerpiece of this costume is a natty wrapping paper hat, over-sized enough for any Hollywood ego. A dress-up box or trip to the thrift store can provide the rest: sunglasses, a killer gown, and sparkling faux gems. And don't forget the most important accessory of all — a pack of equally glamorous pals.

MATERIALS

3 25- to 30-inch square sheets of wrapping paper or tissue paper
Glue stick
Masking tape
Hat decorations (crepe paper, ribbon, fake flowers, gift bows, pipe cleaners, fabric, and feathers)
Assorted dress-up clothes including fancy shoes and faux jewelry

The hat: Glue the three sheets of paper together in the center. Have the print or color of the bottom sheet facedown, so the underside of the hat will be patterned too. **1** To form the hat's crown, center the paper on top of your child's head and gently press the edges of the paper down around the sides of her head. Wrap masking tape around the crown (at eyebrow level) two to three times. Create the brim by rolling the paper edges up or under and taping in place, or by trimming the edges. Decorate with flowers, bows, ribbons, crepe paper, pipe cleaners, fabric scraps, feathers, or plastic tiaras — whatever accessorizes your child's party dress best.

Dress-up: After putting on her party dress, jewelry, sunglasses, and shoes, your child can don her new chapeau and get ready for the rave reviews.

FACE PAINT

Clown Around

You can put on this jolly clown face in minutes — about the same time it will take most kids to slip into character and start clowning around. Start with a damp sponge and apply white face paint to your child's entire face, including his eyebrows. Use a small makeup brush to paint his upper and lower eyelids white. Once the base coat dries (it usually takes just a few minutes), brush on facial features: a green diamond and a blue star to accentuate his eyes, a round red nose, and full red lips. Paint on pointy red eyebrows about an inch above his real brows. Finish off the disguise with baggy clothes, a curly wig, and a frilly collar.

Salty Fisherman

He may not be old enough to captain a ship, but netting treats won't be a trick for this old salt. A variation on the movie star hat at left, this fisherman's Gloucester hat is just as easy to make.

First, glue two sheets of yellow wrapping paper together, yellow side down. Form the crown by gently pressing the papers on your child's head and taping the crown to secure. Then glue a third piece of paper on top, yellow side up. Trim the brim to be long in back and short in front. Complete the look by dressing your child in a yellow raincoat and pants, rubber boots, and a store-bought or homemade yarn beard. Don't forget a rod, reel, and net for catching treats.

Motorcycle Rider

If it can move, boys usually like it. Hence their immediate draw to this costume. The trash bag leather vest is just plain cool, as is the cardboard cycle, which lets you throttle past the other tricksters next to you and get to the candy first.

MATERIALS

4 26- by 30-inch pieces and 1 12- by 30-inch piece corrugated cardboard
Double-sided mounting tape
Tempera paints
Paper towel tubes
Aluminum foil
Black trash bag
Masking tape
Poster board
Electrical tape
White T-shirt
Blue jeans
Black shoes
Bandanna

Bike: Sketch a simple side view of the front and back halves of the bike, each on a separate sheet of the 26- by 30-inch pieces of cardboard. Include a 5-inch-wide strip down the forward part of the back of the bike and the rear part of the front. Carefully cut out both shapes, then trace and cut out another copy of each one. **1** Fold in the rectangular panels on both front pieces, affix strips of double-sided tape to one, then press the two panels together. Tape together the front edges of the wheel, too. Repeat for the two rear pieces. **2** Cut the shoulder yoke out of the 12- by 30-inch piece of cardboard as shown, testing to make sure the hole fits over your child's head and neck. **3** Use double-sided tape to attach the yoke to the bike's front and back. Paint the bike. Cut holes for handlebars and footrests (the same diameter as the paper towel tubes). Cover the tubes with foil and insert.

Leather vest: 4 Cut a hole in each top corner of the trash bag for the armholes and one in the center for the collar. "Hem" the sides of the collar and vest with masking tape. Trace the collar onto poster board, then cut out. Make a center cut up the vest front. Turn the vest inside out and insert the poster board in the collar. Add electrical tape zippers and buttons.

Assembly: Have your child put on the T-shirt, shoes, jeans, and bandanna. Slip the cycle yoke over his head so it rests on his shoulders. Put on the vest and throttle the engine.

The Littlest Mermaid

Who says toddlers can't trick-or-treat in style? This glamorous mermaid outfit was designed by *FamilyFun* reader Susan Russo of Riverview, Florida. The wave stroller was added by *FamilyFun* craft experts.

MATERIALS

Mermaid:

>   Peach-colored felt
>   Fabric paint
>   White T-shirt or
>   infant's bodysuit
>   Glue gun
> 1 yard plain teal
>   fabric
>   Insulating foam
>   tube
>   Black tempera paint
>   Thread
>   Ribbon
>   Fiberfill batting

Stroller decorations:

>   48- by 48-inch piece
>   blue microfleece
>   Safety pins
> 1 yard blue satin
>   fabric
>   Fiberfill batting
>   Sponges, bubble
>   wrap, pipe
>   cleaners

The top: Cut two shells from the peach felt. Draw lines on the shells with fabric paint. When dry, glue the shells to the T-shirt.

The tail: **1** Lay the teal fabric on a flat surface. Cut the foam tube in half, dip one semicircular end into black paint, print scales onto the fabric, and let dry. Draw a fish tail pattern on paper (make it extra long; your child's feet should just reach to the narrowest part of the tail), then cut out two matching tails from the fabric. Sew them together inside out, then sew a hem at the top of the tail and turn the tail right side out. Thread a piece of ribbon through the hem for a drawstring. Fill the tail end with fiberfill.

The stroller: Drape microfleece over the stroller and safety-pin the fabric in place. Cut holes to accommodate the stroller straps. **2** To make a wave top for the stroller, sew a blue satin hood with a wavy bottom edge. Stuff with fiberfill batting, then slip over the stroller top. If you wish, decorate the stroller with sea life: fishes made of sponges, jellyfish made of bubble wrap, and sea horses made of pipe cleaners.

Assembly: Dress your little mermaid in her top and tail and stroll away.

Fairy Princess

Glinda the Good Witch can't hold a candle to a little girl decked out in this fairy princess costume. Take your princess-to-be to a craft store and pick up the Model Magic, craft foam, Styrofoam egg, and puff paint. The other items can be found at a fabric store or around the house.

MATERIALS
Wand:
    12-inch dowel
    Purple acrylic paint

4 15-inch pink and silver ribbons
    Rubber band
    Styrofoam egg
    White Model Magic compound
    Plastic rhinestones, beads, or sequins

Shirt:
    Lavender turtleneck
    Glitter puff paint
1½ yards lace trim
    Needle and thread or fabric glue
    Small round plastic storage container and small mixing bowl (optional)

Skirt:
2 yards of 2-inch-wide ribbon
2 yards each pink, light purple, and iridescent tulle
    Needle, pins, and pink thread
    Silver rickrack
2 self-adhesive Velcro fasteners
    Purple tights

Crown:
1 yard pink tulle
    Pink craft foam, 11 by 17 inches
    2-inch-wide lace trim
2 feet of elastic cord
    Silver ribbon

Wand: **1** Paint the dowel and let it dry. Fold the ribbons in half, then place the fold at the tip of the dowel and wrap with the rubber band to attach.

Push this end into the base of the Styrofoam egg. Flatten a 2-inch ball of Model Magic to ⅛-inch thickness. Wrap it around the egg completely, then trim excess and smooth the clay with your fingertips. Push the plastic gemstones into the clay and dry overnight.

Shirt: **2** Lay the turtleneck flat, then squeeze puff paint dots along the sleeves and the body. Once dry, repeat on the other side. Next, glue or stitch the lace trim to the sleeves and the turtleneck. To make this process easier, insert a plastic storage container into the sleeve and a bowl into the turtleneck before stitching or gluing, as shown.

Skirt: **3** Cut the ribbon into two lengths: 30 inches for the waistband and 42 inches for the bow. Next, fold each length of tulle in half lengthwise and stack them on top of each other, folded edges together. Using a needle and a 40-inch-long piece of thread, hand-stitch across the top of the skirt through all the layers of fabric. When you're done, hold the thread end in one hand and gather fabric together with the other until it fits onto the 30-inch waist ribbon. Pin the top of the

skirt to the ribbon, distributing the gathers evenly. Hand-stitch the ribbon and fabric together, then remove the pins. Trim the outer skirt layer with silver rickrack; stitch in place. To fit the skirt, wrap the waistband around your child's waist, mark where the ends fall, and secure with self-adhesive Velcro fasteners. Tie a bow in the center of the 42-inch ribbon and glue or stitch it to the waistband.

Crown: **4** Knot one end of the tulle, then place it in the center of the craft foam sheet, as shown. Roll either side of the foam into the center to make a cone and staple together (the top staple will secure the tulle). Trim the bottom of the cone as shown. Sew or glue the lace trim around the bottom edge. Knot both ends of the elastic cord and staple them to either side of the inside of the hat. Run silver ribbon around the top of the cone and spiral down the entire length of the cone; glue in place.

Assembly: Now it's time for the princess to get dressed. First, have her put on the lacy turtleneck and tights. Then wrap the skirt around her waist, put on the crown, and — ta da! — hand her the magic wand.

LEGO-Lover

The only thing better than building with a LEGO is being dressed up like one for Halloween. That's what dozens of LEGO maniacs said after seeing the directions for this creative costume in *FamilyFun* magazine. The original design came from 11-year-old Bryan Hartley of Richmond, Virginia.

MATERIALS

Large cardboard box (find one that's close to your child's shoulder width)

7 margarine containers or plastic cups (see Crafter's Tip, right)

Hot glue gun

Small shallow box that fits your child's head

Spray paint

Baseball cap

Double-sided tape

Gloves

Sweat suit

The body: Measure the circumference of your child's head, then use a utility knife to cut a head opening in the top of the box approximately 2 inches from the front edge. Cut an armhole near the top front corner on each side of the box. Have your child try the box on so you can make any adjustments. **1** Now arrange the margarine containers on the front of the box, as shown, and trace around each one. Using the hot glue gun (parents only), apply glue around one of the circles, then press the margarine container in place. Repeat for five other containers. **2** Glue an additional container on top of the smaller box for the hat. Spray-paint both boxes.

The hat: Have your child put the baseball cap on backward, then apply double-sided tape to the top of it. Fit the small box on top so it just covers the bottom edge of the back of the hat.

Crafter's Tip: Like real LEGO toys, this costume can be made in different configurations, depending on the size of the box and the cups you use. Here, we've shown the costume created with margarine tubs so it looks like one king-size LEGO piece. In Bryan's original version, he glued on 32 bathroom cups, then delineated eight "bricks" with black marker.

The cap: **1** Trace the baseball hat visor onto orange felt twice, leaving a 1-inch margin around the front and sides. Cut out the shapes, then glue to the top and underside of the visor (they'll overlap a bit). From the black felt, cut four dime-size circles. Glue two to the visor for nostrils and the other two to the white pom-poms for eyeballs. Glue the pom-poms to the front of the hat.

The feet: **2** Trace your child's sneakers onto orange felt, leaving a 1-inch margin. Cut out the shapes, adding three webbed toes to each. Fold the feet in half lengthwise and cut an asterisk into the back center of each foot as shown, leaving a ¾-inch margin around the opening. Apply Velcro strips to the bottoms of the duck feet and the tops of the orange socks.

Body: **3** Shape batting into a thick cylinder as wide as your child's waist and tape it inside the back of the sweatshirt. Cut three tail feathers, about 12 inches long, from the yellow and white felt.
4 To make the wings, cut two rectangles of white felt about 20 inches by 8 inches. Fold each in half and trace a simple wing pattern onto the felt. Cut out the pattern, as shown, then glue the wing tips together, leaving a wide sleeve for your child's arm.

Assembly: Put on the leggings and the white turtleneck. Next, put on the duck feet, then the sneakers with socks over them. Last, put on the sweatshirt and tape the tail feathers to the back with cloth tape. Slip on the wings and hat.

Mr. Postman

Eric Mattingly, a five-and-a-half-year-old *FamilyFun* fan from Lexington, Kentucky, came up with a mailbox costume all by himself. All he and his parents used to make it was a large cardboard box, a few sheets of poster board, and royal blue and white paint. His mom and dad report that on the big night, Eric was proud to pick up special deliveries around the neighborhood.

Scarecrow

A flock of cute crows (made from toddler socks) roosts on this classic scarecrow costume. This sweet fellow is stuffed with soft straw cut from craft foam, which is available at craft stores for about $1 a sheet.

MATERIALS

Scarecrow:
- 1 sheet each of beige, yellow, and brown craft foam
- 3 large calico fabric "patches"
- Denim overalls
- Safety pins
- Yellow turtleneck
- Striped socks
- Flannel plaid shirt
- Work gloves
- Work boots
- Self-adhesive Velcro squares
- Canvas or straw hat

Crows:
- 2 pairs black toddler socks
- Fiberfill batting
- 12 black feathers
- Fabric glue or needle and thread
- Yellow construction paper scraps
- 8 googly eyes
- 2 yellow pipe cleaners

Scarecrow straw:

1 Cut three 4-inch-wide strips out of the beige craft foam: two that are long enough to fit around your child's wrists, and one that will fit comfortably around his neck. Next, cut a wavy edge along the top of all the foam strips to give the straw an uneven appearance. Then fringe the top of each, leaving the bottom inch intact, as shown. Make straw for stuffing into the scarecrow's pockets by cutting thin strips of all the craft foam colors.

Patched overalls:

Arrange the calico fabric patches on the knees and front pocket of the overalls and pin them in place.

Baby sock crows:

2 Use one black sock for each bird. The toe will become the head, the heel will be its belly, and the cuff will be its tail. **3** Stuff each sock with batting, then poke a black feather into the cuff. Fold the cuff around the feather and either stitch or glue the cuff closed. To make the beak, fold a yellow paper scrap in half and cut out a triangle along the fold line (when you open the beak it should be a diamond shape). Glue the fold of the beak and a pair of googly eyes to the toe of the sock. Poke half a yellow pipe cleaner through the heel of the sock, then fold each end into a foot shape. Glue feather wings to the sides of each bird.

Assembly: Have your child put on the turtleneck, striped socks, and flannel shirt. Next, slip on the gloves, patched overalls, and work boots and roll up the overall cuffs. Wrap the finished "straw bands" around his wrists, ankles, and neck and attach with the Velcro square closures. Stuff the extra straw into the pockets of his overalls and shirt. **4** Glue straw onto the hat. Finally, pin each bird by its belly to the hat, overall pocket, shoulder, and glove.

Wicked Witch

She might take it as an insult, but the Queen of Halloween has never looked so good. From her fiendish fingernails to her towering newspaper hat, she's simply spellbinding.

MATERIALS

    Newspaper
    Masking tape
    Black electrical tape
    Black paint
    Cardboard
    Aluminum foil
 1- by 2-yard piece of
     black gauze
     fabric
    Black ribbon
10 water picks (available at florists)
    Wig, rubber snake, striped socks, and other accessories

The hat: ◼1 Roll a tall newspaper cone and secure with masking tape. Roll up the bottom edge until it fits your child's head. ◼2 For the hat brim, use three sheets of newspaper. Roll in the outer edges, taping them in place so that you create a circle with a rolled edge. Trace the cone bottom onto the center of the brim, then, as shown, divide that circle like a pie, cutting along the center lines. Push the cone up through the brim and tape in place. Paint the hat black. Cut out a cardboard buckle, cover with foil, and secure with black tape to the front of the hat.

The robe: ◼3 Fold the fabric in half so the short ends meet, then cut an approximately 7-inch hole for your child's head. Have her slip on the robe, then you can cut a fringy edge in the bottom. Belt with a black ribbon.

Assembly: Stick on water picks for fingernails, add accessories and the witch hat, and she's ready to fly around the neighborhood.

A Smashing Pumpkin

Dressed warmly as the veggie of the season, your child will stand out in any crowd — or pumpkin patch. The sturdy hat is made of chair foam, which is available at fabric stores.

MATERIALS
Hat:

	2- to 3-inch-thick foam chair pad
	Serrated knife
	Acrylic paint (brown and orange)
1	**square each of light green and dark green felt**
2	**green pipe cleaners**
	Needle and thread
	22 inches of ¼-inch-thick elastic band
	Glue

Suit:

2	**yards of 36-inch-wide orange felt**
	Orange thread
54	**inches of ½-inch-wide elastic band**

Green leggings
Green turtleneck
Large green socks
Newspaper
Fiberfill batting (optional)

The hat: Sketch an outline of a pumpkin top on the foam. With a serrated knife, cut the lid out so that the top is wider than the bottom. With scissors, sculpt the top of the lid so that it slopes down in the center. Next, round the underside of the hat to fit your child's head. Paint the the sides and top of the hat orange. Carve a foam stem and paint it brown. For the leaf, cut an identical leaf shape out of both colors of green felt and sew them together. For tendrils, twist two pipe cleaners together, then curl the ends. Sew one of the tendrils to the underside of the leaf. Glue the foam stem and leaf to the center of the hat. Cut a chin strap out of elastic band and sew it to the hat.

The suit: 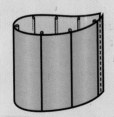 Make the pumpkin out of the orange felt. First, draw a vertical line, in the short direction, every 6 inches, on the felt. Fold along each marked line as shown. With orange thread, sew a ¼ inch seam from each fold. Fold the felt in half lengthwise with the lines facing in and sew the ends together to make a tube. Fold over a 1-inch casing at the top and bottom of the suit and sew. Cut the ½-inch elastic band into a 22-inch and a 32-inch length (for the top and bottom casings, respectively). Insert the elastic into the casings, then sew the ends of the bands together. Turn the suit right side out and cut armholes to fit your child.

Assembly: Have your child put on the leggings, turtleneck, and green socks over his regular shoes. Put on the suit and stuff the pumpkin with crumpled newspaper (you can place a layer of batting around the inside to soften the newspaper). Finally, put on the pumpkin patch hat.

CHAPTER THREE

Haunted House Party

THE COOLEST PARENTS on the block are always the ones who host the Halloween party. They give the thumbs-up to slimy messes, gross masks, creepy games, and party food that moves. They don't mind a cobweb that never quite rubs off the doorjamb or wince at screams coming from behind their drapes. They even enjoy little partygoers who are a bit wired on sugar and anticipation.

If you're the Halloween hosts this year, we have dozens of party crafts, games, and activities that will be the hit of your Halloween party. All of the ideas are easy to pull off and have been tested by the readers of *FamilyFun* magazine. The tips below will help you create a successful party structure — and keep you from turning into a party-planning monster.

Start planning early. The best Halloween parties take time to plan, so begin about a month in advance for a nonstressful pace. Invite your kids to help you with all aspects of the party arrangements, from writing a guest list to choosing the games and activities. To a child, getting ready for the party can be as much fun as the day itself.

Make your Halloween bash age-appropriate. Remember to consider the ages of the invitees — one child's thrill is another child's nightmare. If you plan on hosting mixed ages, set up spooky activities for older kids, such as the Monster Operation on page 69, in a spare

room. In another room, set up some not-so-scary activities for little kids, such as painting pictures of pumpkins.

Choose a lineup of activities. For a two-hour party, plan more events than you think you will need. Start with a welcome activity, such as the Sign-in Mural on page 64, then alternate quiet crafts with active games. End with Halloween cake or another sweet surprise and a ghost storytelling session.

Plan a ghoulish menu. On Halloween, kids fill up on candy, so it's important to balance sweets with a nutritious menu. Try some *FamilyFun* favorites, such as Skeleton Crude-itay on page 78, Hot Dog Worms, page 86, or Scary Face Pizzas, page 84.

Set up a spooky space. Moody lighting, haunting music, and some all-important pumpkins will set the scene for your Halloween bash. If you want to spook up your house even more, include some decoration-making activities on your party agenda (see "Spooky Crafts and Decorations" on page 6 for ideas). Avoid anything with a flame and keep in mind that kids plus costumes equals clumsiness — anything fragile or sharp should be out of the way of the partygoers.

Go with the flow. Once the party begins, don't be afraid to repeat a game that was a huge hit — or scratch one you think won't go over well now that you know the mood of the party. Follow your basic party structure, but remain flexible. Most importantly, relax and have fun.

Eyeball on a Spoon, page 67

Sign-in Mural

GETTING READY
Party Menu

A Halloween party just isn't a party without a buffet of creepy cuisine. Here's our favorite menu:

Skeleton Crude-itay,
    page 78
Spider Pretzels, page 79
Hot Dog Worms, page 86
Witch's House Cake, page 93

Ghoulish guests tend to arrive at different times — and they may not know one another — so ease them into the party with this icebreaker art project.

MATERIALS
    Butcher paper,
        poster board, or
        newsprint
    Tape
    Markers

Tape a large sheet of the butcher paper, poster board, or newsprint at kids'-eye level on a wall where the main activities will take place.

Before guests arrive, use markers to draw a large haunted house at the center of the paper and decorate it with bats, pumpkins, and other Halloween symbols, leaving lots of room surrounding it for additional art.

Leave out your markers; as the children arrive, ask them to add their costumed self-portraits to the scene and sign their names. The mural will act as an activity — and a party decoration.

Mummy Wrap

Not every Halloween surprise has to go bump in the night. This simple unwrapping game pleases with quieter thrills.

MATERIALS

Roll of toilet paper
10 small prizes, such as plastic critters, small erasers, or tiny candies (1 per guest)

Before the party, tape a small, lightweight prize to the end of a roll of toilet paper. Wrap up the prize in the toilet paper and continue taping prizes and wrapping them until the roll is completely wrapped.

At party time, ask players to sit in a circle. Each person gets to wrap the end of the toilet paper around a body part (an arm, forehead, waist,

ankle, and so on) until she finds a prize. She then tears the paper and passes the roll to the next player.

Play continues until all the prizes have been unrolled. Let kids keep the gifts as party favors.

MY GREAT IDEA
Ghost Invitations

For her kids' Halloween party, *FamilyFun* reader Tracey Hodapp of Erie, Pennsylvania, came up with a creative invitation idea: footprint ghosts. Using her 11-month-old's foot and washable white paint, she stamped prints on black paper. Turned upside down, the prints looked like ghosts. She then added paper eyes and drew a mouth on each ghost, glued them on cards, and decorated them with stickers.

Haunting Your House

Besides creepy jack-o'-lanterns, every haunted house should have a few of the following:

- **A spooky sound track:** purchase a sound effects cassette or tape a homemade version (clanking chains, screams, howls, crazy laughter, and heavy footsteps)
- **Fake spiderwebs: for a homespun version, see page 66**
- **Plastic insects**
- **Monster footprints: cut big paws out of poster board and tape them to the floors**
- **A mummy-wrapped scarecrow**
- **A vase of dead flowers**
- **Furniture covered with sheets**
- **Black lights shining on glow-in-the-dark creatures**
- **Helium balloon ghosts: drape balloons with sheets and tie at the neck**
- **Sinister signs: hang spooky sayings, such as "Enter at your own risk" and "Experiment in progress"on doors**
- **Fog and smoke: If you feel like splurging, rent an electric fog machine from a party store (cost: about $50)**

DECORATION
Doorway Spider-web

Oh, what a tangled web we wove — and it's infested with spooky Styrofoam spiders. Scared? Don't be. It's actually quite easy to make.

MATERIALS

For each spider:
- Black tempera paint
- Paintbrush
- 2 Styrofoam balls, one slightly smaller than the other
- Toothpicks
- 8 black pipe cleaners
- Red construction paper

Web:
- Thick gray yarn
- Tape or tacks
- Water

First, make the spiders for the web. Help your child paint the Styrofoam balls black and let them dry. Attach the head (smaller ball) to the body (larger ball) with toothpicks. Insert the pipe cleaner legs into the body and bend them in half to create the knee joints. Bend the tips to create the feet. Now give the spider a frightening face by

gluing on two paper triangle eyes, as shown.

Next, make the web. First, run a length of yarn across the top of a doorframe and tape or tack in place. Just before your guests arrive, wet (but don't soak) a dozen or so 6-foot-long strands of yarn and gently pull each strand apart to create a cobweb effect. Drape them over the yarn on the door frame. Suspend a few spiders on the web by twisting the pipe cleaner legs around the yarn. For maximum chills, invite your guests to walk through the doorway, brushing against the wet web as they walk.

For best results, keep a spray bottle of water on hand for respraying the cobweb when it dries out.

Eyeball on a Spoon

Try this creepy variation on the wholesome egg-on-a-spoon race.

MATERIALS
> Ping-Pong balls
> Markers
> Teaspoons

Make eyeballs in advance (one per guest) by drawing an iris, a pupil, and bloodshot veins onto Ping-Pong balls.

To play, set up a starting and a finish line. Hand each child an eyeball on a spoon. At the whistle, the kids must race to the finish line without touching their eyeball. If it falls, the player must retrieve the eyeball and return to the starting line and begin again; whoever makes it to the finish line first wins.

Slime Factory

In the house's laboratory — er, kitchen — let party guests watch a mad scientist (Mom or Dad) transform ordinary ingredients into a ghoulish concoction. When guests get their hands on this gross stuff, it oozes delightfully through their fingers.

Here's the magic formula: mix 3/4 cup warm water, 1 cup Elmer's glue, and several drops of green food coloring in a medium-size bowl.

In a separate large bowl, mix 4 teaspoons borax and 1 1/3 cups warm water. This brew will act as the fixative. (Note: Since borax is toxic in large doses, be sure to keep this mixture away from kids younger than age three.)

Pour the glue mixture into the borax and water mixture, but do not stir. Let it sit for 1 minute, then lift the congealed slime out of the liquid. Divide it up so that each child has his or her own piece of slime to play with.

Keep in mind that the glue in this slime can make it stick to certain fabrics. To minimize accidents, give each little monster a sealable bag to store his slime in.

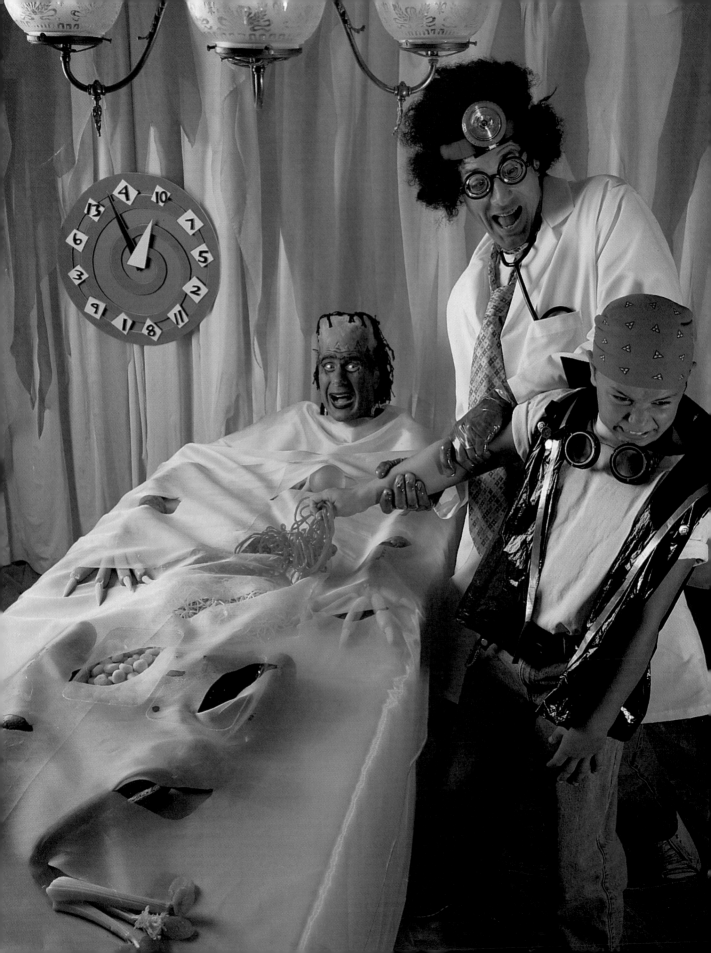

HALLOWEEN TRICK

Monster Operation

In this gooey game, a parent dressed as a monster sits at the end of an operating table as young physicians (party guests) examine his ghoulish guts.

MATERIALS

> Zucchini, turnip, celery, dried apricots, baby corn, hot dogs, cooked spaghetti, licorice ropes, prepared gelatin, water chestnuts
> Toothpicks
> Thumbtacks
> Plastic pie plate
> Water balloon
> Duct tape
> Old sheets or shower curtains

To make the monster's body, arrange vegetables on a picnic table to resemble a skeleton, minus the head (the head, after all, belongs to the parent). For arms, thighs, and shins, use zucchini; a turnip, split in half, makes excellent kneecaps. Use toothpicks to pin a celery rib cage together; secure dried apricot toes to celery feet; and attach baby corn fingernails to hot dog fingers. Just below the rib cage, pile cooked spaghetti (small intestines) and licorice ropes (large intestines) directly on top of the table. With a thumbtack, secure a plastic pie plate to the picnic table below the intestines. Fill with gelatin (guts). Water chestnut gallstones and a water balloon heart make nice additions to the monster.

When the organs are in place, secure them to the table with duct tape.

Top the operating table with an old sheet or shower curtain and cut slits in it so the children can reach in and touch the organs without being able to see them.

Just before the costumed kids arrive, position the live monster (a parent with green face paint) at the head of the table, sitting on a chair. To create the illusion that the head is connected to the body, drape a second sheet over the monster's shoulders.

When the kids arrive, explain that the monster needs an extensive checkup, requiring the kids' help. Guiding their hands through the slits, instruct them to tweak, prod, and poke at his guts.

When you announce the patient needs a complete overhaul, the monster suddenly rises from his chair and roars.

HALLOWEEN TRICK

Frankenfinger

Poke a hole in the bottom of a small box, lay in some cotton or other filler as shown, and push your finger up through. Leave the lid on until the party guests are just dying to see what's inside. Then open the box with a flourish. Oh, what a scream!

Fishing for Fortunes

This fun-loving fortune-telling session employs tasty tokens, which double as a take-home treat.

MATERIALS
Take-home treats and prizes
Goldfish bowl

Magic Wanda (a parent dressed as a gypsy) invites children to her private, velvet-covered fortune-telling table in the corner of the room. One by one, Wanda asks children to close their eyes and retrieve a take-home treat from her crystal ball (a goldfish bowl) in the cen-

ter of the table. Based on the item, Wanda predicts the child's future: a chocolate coin equals a raise in allowance; a gummy rat foretells a pet in the child's future; a chocolate soccer ball means fame to come in the sports world; a candy pacifier indicates a new sibling; a chocolate

medallion points to a future Olympian.

Testers' Tip: Make sure all the goodies are true treats. One child tester didn't appreciate the travel-size tube of toothpaste ("You'll never have another cavity!") when her friend was devouring chocolate coins.

Cookie Contest

How about this for Halloween magic? Hang these cookies across the room, and they'll act as a party decoration, a treat, and a game.

MATERIALS

- 1 **20-ounce package refrigerator sugar cookie dough**
- **Cookie cutters**
- **Drinking straw or chopstick**
- **String or fishing line**
- **Frosting (optional)**
- **Clothesline**

First, bake the cookies. Heat the oven to 350°. Roll out the cookie dough to a ¼-inch thickness and cut with cookie cutters (we used stars and moons, but you might try Halloween shapes instead). Arrange the cookies on an ungreased cookie sheet. Poke holes through the tops using a straw or chopstick and bake for 7 to 11 minutes or until lightly brown. Two minutes before the cookies come out of the oven, repoke the holes to make sure they are large enough for threading a string. Remove the cookies from the pan and cool on a cooling rack.

Thread the cookies with 2- to 3-foot lengths of string or fishing line. Frost the cookies, if desired.

String the clothesline across the room (preferably the basement, porch, or another room where you don't mind getting crumbs on the floor). Then hang the cookies on the line so they fall at the height of the kids' shoulders. If you're hosting a variety of ages, be sure to hang the strings in different lengths.

To play, instruct the kids to keep their hands behind their backs while they eat the cookies. The first child to eat his entire cookie without it falling to the floor wins. Everyone wins a prize — their cookie.

ACTIVE GAME

Zombie Tag

This game involves the ultimate "it" — a hideous, groaning zombie whose goal is to clutch ... er, tag ... his victims. Our partyers played until they were ready to drop. None of them could resist taunting the blindfolded zombie and toying with fate.

Set up this game in an open area outside or in a large rec room inside. Rope off a circular area or lay down some sweatshirts in a circle and be prepared to yell "Out of bounds!" to your blindfolded zombie. Make sure it's a trip-proof playing area.

To play, follow the classic rules of Marco Polo. "It" wears a rubber monster mask (with a blindfold) and rubber hands. Everyone has to stay within the circle while he wanders around with his arms stretched out in front, zombie style (this also keeps him from crashing). When "it" groans, all the players must groan back and extend their arms. This is how the zombie zeroes in on his victims. When a player gets tagged, she becomes the next "it" and gets to wear the mask and hands.

Grab the Ghost

Who's the ghost with the most? This game of quick reflexes and steady nerves lets you find out.

MATERIALS
- Paper towels
- Small balls
- Yarn
- Markers
- Pennies
- Large paper circle
- Large funnel
- Die

Before the party, make ghosts by draping a piece of paper towel around a small ball, such as a Superball (or in a pinch, a wadded-up paper towel). Cinch the towel around the ball and secure with one end of a 2-foot length of yarn. Have guests draw a face on their ghosts with markers.

At the start of the game, each player is given ten pennies. Choose one person to be the goblin. The other players lay their ghosts on the large paper circle and hold on to the yarn leash. The goblin holds the funnel, upside down, at least 2 feet above the circle.

The goblin chooses two numbers on a die, announces them to the group, then rolls. If either of the chosen numbers appears, the players try to pull their ghosts out of the circle before the goblin can slam the funnel down over them. If a player is caught, he must give the goblin a penny. If the chosen numbers do not appear, but the players panic and yank their ghosts out of the circle anyway, it's another penny to the goblin. The goblin, for his part, is allowed to fake a funnel slam, but if he touches any ghost, he must shell out a penny to each player.

After three rolls of the die, the next player takes over as goblin. Play is over when one player runs out of pennies. The player with the most coins wins. As a prize, let him keep his pile of pennies.

Witch's Stew

This game requires skill, speed, and raw straw-sucking power. To train, we suggest slurping up a thick milk shake or two.

Before the party, ask your children to help you cut out ten Halloween shapes, such as ghosts, bats, and pumpkins, from construction paper. Each shape should be about the size of a yo-yo.

Place the shapes in a pile beside a small bowl. Using the straw as a vacuum, each contestant should try to pick up a shape and place it in the bowl to create the Witch's Stew.

Time the players to see who can get all ten in the bowl fastest. For a head-to-head race, cut out two sets of the shapes and let the players race against each other.

MY GREAT IDEA
Halloween Twister

FamilyFun reader **Deborah Lee-Quinn of Belleville, Illinois, made this truly twisted party**

game, a Halloween version of Twister. Using fabric paint, sons Jonathan and Erik helped their mom paint rows of cats, bats, pumpkins, and ghosts on a 4- by 4-foot piece of felt, then made a corresponding spinner out of poster board. With five kids playing Halloween Twister, it was a tangled web of arms and legs.

PARTY FAVOR
Spider Pops

When we ran these leggy lollipops in *FamilyFun* magazine, there were spiders, spiders everywhere. One reader, Patti Ummel of Bartlett, Illinois, hatched dozens of them for her child's second grade Halloween party (see photo below).

For each one, you'll need 4 black pipe cleaners, a lollipop, googly eyes, and glue. Hold all four pipe cleaners, center them at the base of the pop, and wrap them around the stick once so there are four legs on each side. Bend the legs as shown. Glue on googly eyes. Now, is it a trick — or treat?

ACTIVE GAME
Spider Relay Race

Here's a takeoff on crab races, perfect for exhausting some of your party crew's energy.

MATERIALS
    4 old pairs of black or
       striped tights
    2 belts
       Fiberfill batting

First, make a set of four spider legs for each team; you can make each set by stuffing 2 pairs of tights and tying them together. Tie them to a belt, which will buckle behind each player's back.

Set up the relay race in a big open rec room or the yard. Outside, you can set up safe (soft) obstacles with hay or straw bales, then spread out a pile of leaves for a finish line.

To play, divide your partyers into two teams and mark a finish line about 20 yards off for big kids (make it closer if you are playing with kids under age seven).

The first player on each team straps a set of legs around her waist so that two legs will dangle on each side of her when she's in the classic crab position. On "Go!" the first players scurry on all fours (well, eights), with their bellies to the sky, to the finish line and back (note: longhaired girls, beware of stomping on your own hair!).

Each team then helps its player take off the spider legs before strapping them onto the next player, who "runs" the race and returns. This continues until the final player from each team comes across the finish line.

PARTY FAVOR
Freaky Hair

This activity will make your hair stand on end. Spread out a white sheet on the floor or on a bed, then have a child lie down on it. Help the child fan out his or her hair (have a wig on hand for the crew-cut contingent). Invite the child to make his or her most gruesome Halloween face, while you take a Polaroid picture from directly above. When the photo develops, write the child's name on it, use it as a place card for the party table, and then send it home as a party favor.

LIZZIE

SECRET INGREDIENTS

1 TOAD
5 VULTURE FEATHERS
7 POISON IVY LEAVES
4 DRAGON TEARS

3 CAT EYES
9 RED ANTS
10 SHARK'S TEETH
6 PIG TAILS

ACTIVE GAME

Witches' Brew

What are those crabby, old witches cooking up this time? Uncovering the recipe is an uproarious task in this game.

MATERIALS
    Construction paper
    Markers

    Double-sided tape
    Soup pot or cauldron

    Let's say you have eight kids playing. To set up, each child will need his or her own color-coded, matching set of eight ingredients (use colored paper and markers): child #1 has eight green copies of one toad, child #2 has eight brown copies of five vulture feathers, and so on. With double-sided tape, affix seven copies to each child's back (the eighth is his or hers to hold) and set out the pot. On "Go!" the players must try to protect their own backs while pulling off one ingredient from each of the other players. The first to collect all eight ingredients puts them in the pot of witches' brew.

Witch's House Cake, page 93

CHAPTER FOUR

Creepy Cuisine

FROM A COOK'S PERSPECTIVE, preparing for Halloween used to be a snap: all you had to do was open a bag of store-bought candy, pour it into a bowl, and wait for the ghosts and ballerinas in your neighborhood to ring the doorbell. But these days, with neighborhood parties and costume parades, making the treat has gotten trickier. At each event, the little monsters are hungry for some creepy cuisine. And you want to offer them a lot more than a bowl of candy to satisfy their appetites.

In this chapter, you'll find many Halloween recipes that have been tested and heartily approved by our own group of trick-or-treaters. Some of them may look a little scary, but they're not difficult to prepare — especially if you follow these cooking tips from the kitchen witches at *FamilyFun*.

Get the kids into the kitchen. It may be easier and less messy to prepare the recipes on your own, but the kids will miss out on the fun. Let them flip through the pages in this chapter and choose a few to try. And even if the recipes don't turn out perfectly, the kids will still feel proud of their creations.

Be prepared. A few weeks before Halloween, stock up on orange and black food coloring to add to cookies and frostings (for the most vibrant colors, buy food coloring paste, available at party and kitchen supply stores). Also, pick up some Halloween-themed cookie cutters, such as a bat, witch, or pumpkin.

Balance Halloween candy with nutritious foods. Before your kids head out for a night of trick-or-treating, let them fill up on something healthy. Try Tomato Soup with Goop, page 78, a Snake Sandwich, page 85, or the Skeleton Crude-itay on page 78.

Send a creepy snack to school. One mom we know sent all the ingredients for making the Spider Pretzels on page 79 to her child's preschool class. At snacktime, the kids had as much fun making the snack as they did eating it.

Inspect Halloween treats. For safety reasons, remind your kids to wait until they get home from trick-or-treating before they eat their candy. That way, you can check each piece.

Label Halloween treats. Homemade treats usually aren't a good idea for trick-or-treating, but if you would like to make some instead of buying candy, here's a tip: package the treats with personalized labels, so everyone knows whose kitchen they came from. If the parents are worried about letting their kids eat the food, they can call you.

Set a spooky table. When serving haunt cuisine, dress up your table. Start with an orange or black tablecloth, then add themed paper napkins, a few of the Pumpkin Candleholders on page 19, and Spider Pops on page 74. Now all you need is some devilish dinner music.

Carrot Cookies, page 91

Skeleton Crude-itay

This guy may look scary, but he could get your kids to eat their vegetables on Halloween.

Assorted fresh vegetables (see photo, right)
2 cups vegetable dip

Build your skeleton on a large platter. Arrange zucchini and squash slices down the center as the spine. Cut two long slices of cucumber and place them as the shoulder bones. Use green beans for arms and cherry tomatoes as the elbows. Use a cauliflower floret for each hand with baby carrot fingers.

Next, arrange rows of celery for the rib cage, red pepper slices for the hip-bones, and carrot slices for the leg bones. From here, create mushroom ankles, broccoli floret feet, and snap pea toes. Finally, fill a hollowed-out cabbage with dip and place it at the "head" of the platter. Serves 10 to 12.

Tomato Soup with Goop

This concoction with strings of melted cheese will warm tricksters on a fall day.

In a food processor or a blender, blend 1 28-ounce can crushed tomatoes with 1 chopped celery stalk, 1/2 chopped large onion, 1 diced garlic clove, and 1 tablespoon chopped fresh parsley until smooth. Transfer the mixture to a large soup pot. Stir in 2 tablespoons butter, 1 tablespoon sugar, 1 tablespoon all-purpose flour, 1 teaspoon seasoned salt, and 1/2 teaspoon pepper. Cook over medium-high heat, stirring occasionally, until the mixture comes to a boil. Reduce the heat to low.

Set out serving bowls and 8 1-ounce sticks of string cheese. Portion out one string torn into strips into each bowl.

A few minutes before serving, pour 3½ cups milk and 1 cup heavy cream into the soup pot and stir thoroughly. Cook briefly over medium heat but do not boil (this will cause the milk and cream to separate). When the soup is steaming, ladle it into the bowls.

Each diner can lift the goop to the surface, play with strings, and eat them too. Serves 8.

QUICK SNACK
Spider Pretzels

These arachnid treats are easy to make — and they look positively lifelike crawling across your child's snack plate.

For each:

- 2 **round crackers**
- 2 **teaspoons smooth peanut butter**
- 8 **small pretzel sticks**
- 2 **raisins**

With the peanut butter, make a cracker sandwich. Insert eight pretzel "legs" into the filling. With a dab of peanut butter, set two raisin "eyes" on top. Makes 1.

SWEET TREAT
Taffy Pull

This recipe is one part activity, one part party food. Kids will get a kick out of pulling, cutting, and shaping the taffy (cooking the sweet concoction is a job for parents only).

- 1½ **cups sugar**
- ¾ **cup light corn syrup**
- ⅔ **cup water**
- ¾ **teaspoon salt**
- 1 **teaspoon vegetable glycerin (sold at most party or natural food stores)**
- 2 **tablespoons butter**
- 2 **teaspoons lemon juice**

In a large saucepan, stir together the sugar, corn syrup, water, salt, and glycerin with a wooden spoon. Cook over medium heat, stirring now and then until a candy thermometer reads 255°. Stir in the butter. Pour the mixture onto a greased flat pan and fold over the edges with a spatula to keep them from hardening.

When the candy is cool enough to handle, brush it with lemon juice. Kids grease their hands with butter, take a lump of taffy, and pull and stretch it until it is light and slightly firm. The longer they stretch, pull, and twist the candy, the more air it will have and the closer to beach taffy it will get. The lump

can then be cut with scissors into bite-size pieces. When cool, wrap in waxed paper. Makes 45 1-inch candies.

MY GREAT IDEA
Ghost Pops

Here's a quick and easy Halloween favor from *FamilyFun* reader Barbara Stockard of Garland, Texas. Barbara wrapped a coffee filter

around a lollipop and tied it with a ribbon. Then her kids, Charlotte, ten, and Brian, 13, drew on a spooky face using felt-tipped markers. The fluted edges of the filter make a stiff skirt, so the ghost looks like it is floating. Barbara says her kids loved assembling a host of these treats for party guests.

QUICK SNACK

Creepy Peepers

PARTY FOOD
Big Dipper

For fun, serve slimy brains (guacamole) in a monster skull (a pumpkin shell decorated with veggie features).

You won't have to egg on your kids to enjoy these edible eyeballs.

1   **egg**
1   **teaspoon mayonnaise**
    Dab of mustard
2   **black olives**

First, place an egg in a small saucepan and cover it with cold water. Bring it to a boil and cook for 1 minute, then turn off the heat. Cover and let sit for 12 minutes. Drain the hot water and run cold water over the shell. Then peel the egg and slice it in half lengthwise. Scoop out the yolk into a bowl and mash it with the mayonnaise, mustard, and a pinch of salt. Spoon the mixture back into the egg white halves and top each with a ripe olive. Serves 1.

Flap Jack-o'-Lanterns

If your kids like pumpkin pie, they'll flip over these tasty pancakes.

- 2 cups all-purpose flour
- 1 tablespoon baking powder
- ½ teaspoon salt
- 2 tablespoons sugar
- 1 teaspoon pumpkin pie spice
- 2 eggs
- 1¾ cups milk
- 3 tablespoons melted butter, plus 1 tablespoon for frying
- ½ cup canned pumpkin

Sift together the flour, baking powder, salt, sugar, and pumpkin pie spice in a large bowl. In a medium bowl, whisk the eggs and milk. Add the 3 tablespoons of melted butter and the pumpkin to the wet ingredients and whisk together. Pour the mixture over the dry ingredients and stir just until blended — a few lumps are okay.

Melt the remaining butter on a griddle over medium-high heat. Then pour ¼ cup of batter for each pancake. When the flapjacks bubble on top, flip and cook until brown on the other side. Serve with triangles of butter and maple syrup. Makes 20.

Spider Salad

One year, *FamilyFun* reader Pam LeBoeuf of Hyannis, Massachusetts, had to make a snack for her son's fourth grade Halloween party. Knowing that the kids would be getting plenty of candy, she came up with a treat that was both healthful and fun. She tossed together cubed cantaloupe and watermelon, sliced strawberries, and grapes, then filled plastic champagne glasses with the fruit salad.

Here's where the trick came in: she topped each fruit cup with a plastic spider ring. She wrapped each in plastic, then tied a ribbon around the stem.

Bat Wings

With a little soy sauce and honey, ordinary chicken wings can be transformed into exotic bat wings. First, combine ½ cup honey, 1 cup soy sauce, 1 cup water, and 2 crushed garlic cloves in a large baking dish, reserving ⅔ cup in a bowl for a dipping sauce. Toss in 2 dozen chicken wings and marinate for at least 1 hour. Broil for 8 minutes on each side, allowing the wings to char slightly. Serve with the bowl of reserved dipping sauce. Serves 8.

Banana Ghosts

Here's a Halloween trick your child will have no trouble pulling off — turning a ripe banana into a Halloween treat. Here's how:

Remove any stringy fibers from the peeled banana, then cut it in half widthwise. Push a Popsicle stick into each half through the cut end, then cover each pop with plastic wrap and freeze until firm (about 3 hours).

Next, place a 1.5-ounce piece of white chocolate candy in a microwave-safe bowl and cook on high until melted (it generally takes about 1 minute). With a butter knife, spread the melted white chocolate on the frozen banana halves.

Set the pops on a waxed-paper-covered dish. Press on candies or currants for eyes and mouths and return the pops to the freezer until ready to serve. Makes 2.

Scary Face Pizzas

Kids won't be able to resist customizing their own scary face pizzas for dinner. Just set out a selection of toppings and watch them make faces. For a party, multiply this six-serving recipe to serve a larger group of guests.

- 6 small pitas or mini pizza breads
- ¾ cup tomato sauce
- 3 cups shredded Mozzarella
  Zucchini rounds
  Mushroom slices
  Green and black olives
  Broccoli florets
  Red and green peppers, sliced in curves
  Tomatoes, chopped or sliced
  Pepperoni slices

Heat the oven to 375°. Position the pitas or pizza breads on a large baking sheet and prick them with a fork. Spread about 2 tablespoons of sauce on each pita or pizza bread and sprinkle on about ½ cup of shredded cheese.

Set out bowls of the toppings from the ingredient list. Then let kids choose their favorite toppings to make creepy faces.

Bake for about 10 minutes or until the cheese has melted and the bread begins to get crispy. Makes 6.

Snake Sandwich

A salami snake, slithering across the table, makes an excellent centerpiece.

1 loaf French bread
14 slices of salami, ham, or other luncheon meat
14 slices of Provolone or American cheese

Mayonnaise
Lettuce
Carrot strips
Broccoli florets
Radish
Red pepper

Make one giant salami and cheese sandwich on the French bread, reserving the heels for later use.

Cut the sandwich into 2-inch pieces. Arrange these in a snake curve on a large platter or cutting board. (Garnish the platter with leafy lettuce first.)

For the snake's head, halve one heel and open it to make the snake's mouth. Wedge two carrot strip "fangs" into the

mouth to hold it open. Cut a piece of red pepper into a tongue shape and set it between the fangs. Add broccoli florets for eyes, radish slits for eyebrows, and red pepper for nostrils. Use the remaining heel at the tip for a tail. Serves 8.

Edible Eyeballs

Jiggly gelatin peepers look (and feel) like real eyeballs. To make a batch, pour 1¼ cups boiling water over 2 3-ounce packets yellow gelatin and stir to dissolve completely. Pour into ice cube trays with rounded bottoms (you should be able to fill two 12-cube trays). Refrigerate for 30 to 45 minutes or until they begin to thicken. Remove the trays from the refrigerator and press a blueberry into the center of each "eyeball." Return the tray to the refrigerator for another 1½ to 2 hours.

To unmold, place the bottom of the tray in warm water for about 15 seconds and run a knife around the edges of each cube. Turn the eyes out on a serving plate and refrigerate until serving time. Makes 24 eyeballs.

Pumpkin Patch Muffins

These moist, wholesome muffins are loaded with vitamin A. For extra flavor, try adding chocolate chips or raisins.

1 cup canned pumpkin
1¼ cups sugar
½ cup water
½ cup vegetable oil
2 eggs
1⅔ cups all-purpose flour
1 teaspoon baking soda
1 teaspoon cinnamon
½ teaspoon salt
½ teaspoon baking powder
¼ teaspoon nutmeg
¼ teaspoon ground cloves

Heat the oven to 350°. In a mixing bowl, combine the pumpkin, sugar, water, vegetable oil, and eggs. Beat until well mixed.

Measure the flour, baking soda, cinnamon, salt, baking powder, nutmeg, and ground cloves into a separate bowl, then stir until combined (a great job for kids). Slowly add the pumpkin mixture to the dry ingredients, stirring until just combined.

Spoon the batter into a 12-cup muffin tin lined with paper baking cups. Bake the muffins for 25 minutes. Cool for at least 10 minutes, then serve them plain, buttered, or with cream cheese. Serve warm. Makes 12 muffins.

Pumpkin-Chocolate Chip Muffins: Stir 1 cup chocolate chips into the batter before scooping it into the muffin tin.

Pumpkin-Raisin Muffins: Stir 1 cup raisins into the batter before scooping it into the muffin tin.

Pumpkin Bread: For a delicious loaf of pumpkin bread, pour the batter into a 9- by 5-inch greased and lightly floured loaf pan. Bake for 60 to 70 minutes or until a toothpick inserted into the center comes out clean.

Pumpkin Seeds

The first pumpkins were grown not for their flesh but for their nutty seeds. And with good reason: they're loaded with vitamins, iron, and protein. Beware: preparing the seeds for toasting is a delightfully slimy activity.

1 **small pumpkin**
2 **tablespoons**
    vegetable oil
  Salt

Use a spoon or ice-cream scoop to remove the seeds from the pumpkin and transfer them to a large bowl. Now for the tough part: separate the seeds from the pumpkin fiber (this is a messy job). To make the process a little easier, fill a bowl with water and let the pumpkin seeds soak. Have a bowl of clean water and a colander nearby.

Heat the oven to 300°. Toss the rinsed pumpkin seeds into a smaller bowl, drizzle with the oil, and sprinkle with salt. Spread the seeds on a cookie sheet and bake for 30 to 40 minutes or until slightly brown. Makes about 2 cups.

Cookie Spooks

Serve this troupe of ghost puppets and watch them disappear in a few quick bites. To make some, you'll need a pencil, cardboard, scissors, a batch of your favorite sugar cookie dough or ready-made cookie dough (available in the refrigerator case at your grocery store), a butter knife, Popsicle sticks, confectioners' sugar, milk, and black string licorice.

First, have your child make a pattern for the cookies by drawing a ghost shape on the cardboard and cutting it out.

On a lightly floured surface, roll out the dough to about ⅛-inch thickness. Lay the pattern on the dough and use a butter knife to cut out ghost shapes (it takes two to make each pop).

Place half the cutouts 2 inches apart on a greased cookie sheet. Lay a Popsicle stick in the center of each one, top with another ghost, and then pinch together the edges of the two layers. Bake for 10 to 12 minutes in a preheated 350° oven. Place the cookies on a rack to cool. Next, spread on a glaze made by mixing 1 cup confectioners' sugar with 2 tablespoons milk. Before the glaze hardens, top off your specters by pressing on eyes and a mouth fashioned from snips of black string licorice.

Monster Paws

Kids can't wait to get their hands on these popcorn-stuffed gloves, recommended by Julie Peters of Lakewood, Colorado. Begin with washed, clear plastic gloves (available at beauty supply stores). Stick one candy corn at the tip of each finger, pointy side up, for fingernails. Fill each glove with popcorn. Tie a bow at the wrist with yarn and they're ready to hand out.

PARTY FOOD

Haunt Cuisine

When your crowd is in the mood for gobblin', serve them the specialty of the haunted house: hot dog worms with putrid punch.

Worms on a Bun
Hot dogs
Hamburger rolls
Ketchup

Cut hot dogs (1 per person) into thin slices (you'll get about four worms per dog). Boil or microwave until the slices curl like wiggly worms. Serve three or four worms to a bun and, for an extra-icky touch, add a few squiggles of ketchup.

Putrid Punch
1 .13-ounce package unsweetened lemon-lime Kool-Aid
1 cup sugar
8 cups water
1 can frozen orange juice concentrate
4 cups ginger ale Orange sherbert

Empty the Kool-Aid into a punch bowl. Add the sugar and water and stir until dissolved. Stir in the juice. Just before serving, add the ginger ale and, if desired, ice cubes with gummy worms frozen inside. Float scoops of sherbert on top. Serves 14.

Creepy Cupcakes

These sweets will appeal to both boys and ghouls. Use a favorite cupcake recipe, then set your kids to work.

Ghost Cupcakes

24 baked cupcakes
24 Nutter-Butter
    cookies
    Chocolate frosting
    Vanilla frosting
    Tube of chocolate
      decorator's icing

Coat each baked cupcake with chocolate frosting and partially insert a Nutter-Butter cookie into the top, as shown. Frost the remaining cookie with vanilla frosting. Draw a spooky expression on each ghost with the decorator's icing. Makes 24.

Spider Cupcakes

2½ cups semisweet
      chocolate chips
¼ cup milk
½ cup chopped
      peanuts
¾ cup dry chow
      mein noodles

24 baked cupcakes
    White frosting

First, make the spiders by combining the chocolate chips and milk in a glass bowl. Microwave on high for 1 to 2 minutes, stirring frequently, until smooth. Stir in the nuts and chow mein noodles. Drop by teaspoons onto waxed paper. Stick on extra noodles for spider legs and chill. Frost the cupcakes white, then top each with a spider. Makes 24.

MY GREAT IDEA

PB & Jack-o'-Lantern

Nancy Chisholm of Bountiful, Utah, and her family found a fun and easy lunch idea for their annual Halloween party — pumpkin-shaped peanut butter and honey sandwiches. Even Nancy's three-year-old, Zachary, helped!

For each, they used two slices of sandwich bread (they even found orange bread in their grocery's bakery), and from one they cut out the pumpkin face using a large jack-o'-lantern cookie cutter (or, Nancy says, you can use a knife). On the other slice they spread the peanut butter and then the honey (or jam). The golden honey casts a shiny glow that gives these lunch treats the look of Halloween.

Haunted Graham Cracker House

If you can't turn your house into a diabolical mansion for Halloween, then use graham crackers to create an equally scary one with a rickety porch, a Keep Out sign, and a graveyard. Buy extra supplies and you can make a complete ghost town to display at a Halloween party.

**Empty cereal box or
cracker box
Cardboard
Aluminum foil
Chocolate frosting
Chocolate graham
crackers**

**Black and orange
candies, such as
black shoestring
and twisted
licorice, candy
corn, orange
candy sticks, Tic
Tacs, M&M's,
and Necco wafers
Marshmallows
Crushed chocolate
cookies**

Arrange the empty box upright on a piece of foil-covered cardboard (you can tape it down to secure it). Tape the top flaps of the box together to form a pitched roof.

Use the frosting to glue the graham crackers onto the sides and roof of the box. Next, fill in the cracks by squeezing the frosting through a pastry bag with a plain tip (you can also use a plastic bag with a small hole cut from the corner). Draw crooked windows and board them up with graham cracker scraps.

Shingle the roof with candy corn, then decorate the rest of the house with orange and black candies. You can add a porch by gluing a graham cracker horizontally to the side of the house; support it with licorice or candy sticks.

For a backyard graveyard, flatten the marshmallows, snip off the sides with scissors, then use frosting to stand them up in the courtyard. Write "Boo" or other spooky sayings on the gravestones with the pastry bag of icing.

As a finishing touch, add a crooked walkway of Necco wafers through the yard to the house and a Keep Out sign on the door. Finally, sprinkle crushed chocolate cookies to make the yard.

Candy Corn Balls

A sprinkling of candy corn makes these popcorn balls an extra-special treat. While boiling the syrup is a job for adults only, shaping the balls is a fun activity for little hands.

To make them, put 12 cups popped popcorn in a mixing bowl large enough to allow for stirring. Mix in 1½ cups candy corn.

Next, fill a medium-size bowl with ice water and set out a cookie sheet or a piece of waxed paper.

Mix ¾ cup brown sugar, ¾ cup corn syrup, 6 tablespoons butter, and ½ teaspoon salt in a 4-quart pot. Bring to a simmer over medium-high heat, stirring constantly. Stop stirring and let the syrup boil until an inserted candy thermometer reaches 275° (a parent's job).

Carefully pour the syrup over the popcorn and stir well with a wooden spoon to evenly coat the kernels and candy. Cool slightly.

Now quickly dip your hands into the ice water and shape the popcorn into 3-inch balls. Place on waxed paper to cool completely. Tightly wrap the balls individually in plastic. Makes 18 to 24.

Carrot Cookies

These cakelike cookies get their bright orange color from carrots — and baking them is a fun cooking project for kids. Young chefs can help measure and mix the ingredients and decorate the cookies to look like jack-o'-lanterns.

Cookies:

- 6 to 8 carrots (enough to make 1 cup cooked and mashed)
- 1 cup butter or shortening
- ⅔ cup sugar
- 2 eggs
- ¼ teaspoon lemon extract
- 1 teaspoon vanilla extract
- 2 cups all-purpose flour
- 2 teaspoons baking powder
- ½ teaspoon salt

Glaze:

- 2 cups confectioners' sugar
- 4 tablespoons orange juice
- Mini chocolate chips (optional)

Peel the carrots and cut them into coins. Cover with water in a saucepan and cook over medium-high heat until soft, about 15 minutes. Drain, then mash the cooked carrots with a potato masher or puree in a food processor or blender. (To save time, you might want to cook the carrots the night before you plan to bake the cookies.)

Heat the oven to 350°. Cream the butter or shortening and sugar with a wooden spoon or an electric mixer. Mix in the eggs, mashed cooked carrots, lemon extract, and vanilla extract.

Sift the flour, baking powder, and salt into a separate bowl. Next, fold the flour mixture into the carrot mixture.

Grease a cookie sheet with cooking spray or butter. Drop teaspoons of the batter onto the greased cookie sheet, 1 inch apart. Bake for 12 to 15 minutes or until set.

While the cookies are baking, mix the glaze. Whisk the confectioners' sugar and orange juice in a medium-size bowl. Once cooled, use a butter knife to frost the cookies, then add chocolate chips to make them look like jack-o'-lanterns, if you like. Makes about 70.

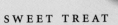

Snake Cake

This sleek-looking snake is easy for kids to help assemble and decorate.

To make one, prepare your favorite cake recipe or boxed mix, then pour the batter into two ring or bundt pans. Bake at 350° for 20 to 30 minutes or until a toothpick inserted into the center comes out clean.

Once cooled, cut the cake rings in half and arrange them in a slithery pattern, frosting them together. Carve a little cake off the sides of the nose, then frost the entire snake (you will need about 5 cups of green frosting in all).

Next, decorate the cake with candies to look like a snake. Add 2 blue gumballs for eyes and a pointy tongue cut from fruit leather. Decorate the rest of the body with yellow candy spots, such as M&M's and nonpareils. Serves 10 to 12.

Wiggly Jiggly Crystal Ball

Let kids gaze into this gelatin crystal ball (packed with cosmic fruit) before helping themselves to a plateful.

In a large, deep bowl, mix 4 3-ounce packages yellow gelatin and 2 envelopes unflavored gelatin. Pour 6 cups boiling water over the mixture and stir until completely dissolved. Refrigerate for 1½ hours or until partially set.

Meanwhile, prepare the cosmic fruit. Cut cantaloupe, watermelon, and green melon into stars and moons with tiny cookie cutters (sets of the cutters or aspic cutters are available in kitchen supply stores for about $16). Press the fruit into the partially set gelatin, then refrigerate for 4 hours or until set.

Place the bowl in a pan of hot water to loosen the gelatin from the sides, then invert onto a wizardlike platter. Serves 16 to 18.

SWEET TREAT
Frozen Witches

Kids will screech with delight over these bewitched desserts. They're just right for a crowd of costumed kids. For best results, make them ahead of time and make room in your freezer.

Tube of chocolate
    decorating gel
8   chocolate cones
8   thin, round
      chocolate wafers
1   pint pistachio ice
      cream
    Black shoestring
      licorice
    Chocolate chips
    Candy corn

To avoid witch meltdowns, make these desserts in batches of four. For each witch hat, squeeze a ring of decorating gel around the edge of a cone and attach the cone to a chocolate wafer "rim," then set it aside.

Using an ice-cream scoop, drop individual "heads" of ice cream onto a cookie sheet lined with waxed paper. Cut licorice to make hair and a mouth and arrange on the ice-cream face. Add chocolate chip eyes and a candy corn nose. Top each scoop with a cone hat. Freeze for 2 hours. Makes 8.

Witch's House Cake

When guests dig into this devilishly delicious cake with its broken candy "glass" path, cookie graveyard, marshmallow ghosts, and spooky hilltop shack, it will be love at first bite.

3 **baked devil's food or chocolate cakes: a 13- by 9- by 2-inch, an 8-inch round cake baked in an ovenproof bowl, and a 6-inch loaf**

4 **cups chocolate frosting**

1 **cup orange frosting Decorations: chocolate graham crackers and ice-cream cones, Nutter Butter cookies, black shoestring licorice, green gumdrops, chocolate kisses, twisted licorice, mini marshmallows, mini chocolate chips, chocolate-covered raisins, and green hard candies**

Cover a large cutting board with foil. Place the 13- by 9- by 2-inch cake on top to create the "graveyard." On one end, place the bowl-shaped cake "hill." Ice the graveyard and hill with chocolate frosting.

Cut out a 2- by 3-inch rectangle, about 1 inch deep, on top of the hill to accommodate the house.

Turn the loaf cake into a house by cutting the corners off one end to make a peaked roof. Place the house in the 2- by 3-inch slot and "paint" the house with orange frosting. Tile the roof with chocolate graham crackers and frosting. Add scary details: windows made of broken chocolate cones with orange icing grids and a peanut butter cookie door with a candy doorknob.

Surround the house with shoestring licorice barbed wire. Add a flying witch (a gumdrop face with a chocolate kiss hat on a twisted licorice broomstick).

To create gravestones, break peanut butter cookies in half and pipe on spooky sayings with orange frosting ("R.I.P.," "Boo," and so on). Secure in the muddy frosting. Next make ghosts in the trees (cut crooked branches in a piece of twisted licorice and add mini marshmallow ghosts with mini chocolate chip eyes), then plant the trees in the mud. Next, draw a crooked path from the base of the cake to the witch's door with a

toothpick. Outline the path with chocolate-covered raisins, then sprinkle with broken green hard candies. At the entrance, add a chocolate graham cracker drawbridge. Finally, outline the yard with broken chocolate cone fencing. Set the house in a place for all to see — and scream about. Serves 20.

Index

Parade of Pumpkins, page 8

A

Activities. *See also* Games, Painting, Quick crafts
  Fishing for Fortunes, 70
  Freaky Hair, 74
  Mummy Wrap, 65
  Sign-in Mural, 64
  Slime Factory, 67
Angel, Heavenly, costume, 39
Animal costumes
  Butterfly Blue, 34
  Dapper Ducks, 56
  dog, 35
  Kitty Cat, 40
  pig, 35
  Roly-Poly Skunk, 35
  sheep, 35
  squirrel, 35
Apple Gals, 11

B

Baby and old lady costume, 38
Banana Ghosts, 82
Bats
  Bat Wings (food), 82
  Clothespin Bats (craft), 8
  Vampire Strikes Back
    (decoration), 16
Blood, Cornstarch, 37
Boxers costume, 42

**Jack-o'-Lanterns,
page 31**

Breakfast, Halloween
  Flap Jack-o'-Lanterns, 81
  Pumpkin Bread, 84
  Pumpkin Patch Muffins, 84
Bubble-blowing Ballplayer, 24
Bug Attack face paint, 47
Bull-riding Cowboy costume, 44
Butler, Headless, costume, 42
Butterfly Blue costume, 34

C

Cakes. *See also* Cupcakes
  Snake Cake, 91
  Witch's House Cake, 93
Candleholders, Pumpkin, 19
Candy Corn Balls, 88
Carrot Cookies, 91
Cats
  black poster board, 9
  costume, 40
Classroom Creep Party, 69
Clown Around face paint, 49
Cookies
  Carrot Cookies, 91
  Cookie Contest, 71
  Cookie Spooks, 85
Costume tips, 33
Cowboy, Bull-riding, costume, 44
Craft tips, 7
Creepy Peepers (food), 80
Cupcakes
  Ghost Cupcakes, 87
  Spider Cupcakes, 87

D

Decorations. *See* individual
  themes (e.g., ghosts), Lawn
  decorations, Porch
  decorations, Table toppers
Desserts. *See* Sweet treats
Dog costume, 35
Doorway Spiderweb, 66
Dr. Frank 'n' Monster costume, 55

E

Eyeballs
  Bulging Eyes (costume), 37
  Creepy Peepers (food), 80
  Edible Eyeballs (food), 84
  Eyeball on a Spoon race, 67

F

Face paint
  Bug Attack, 47
  Clown Around, 49
  Mummy Mug, 37
Fairy Princess costume, 52

Fake Gums and Fangs, 37
Favors. *See* Party favors
Fisherman, Salty, costume, 49
Flap Jack-o'-Lanterns, 81
Food tips, 77
Fortunes, Fishing for, 70
Frankenstein. *See also* Monsters
  Dr. Frank 'n' Monster
    costume, 55
  Frankenfinger, 69
  Frankenstein costume, 47
Freaky Hair, 74
Frozen Witches, 92
Fruits
  Banana Ghosts, 82
  Spider Salad, 81
  Wiggly Jiggly Crystal Ball, 92

G

Games. *See also* Activities
  Cookie Contest, 71
  Eyeball on a Spoon, 67
  Grab the Ghost, 73
  Halloween Twister, 73
  Spider Relay Race, 74
  Witches' Brew, 75
  Witch's Stew, 73
  Zombie Tag, 71
Gelatin
  Edible Eyeballs, 84
  Melting Skin, 37
  Wiggly Jiggly Crystal Ball, 92
Ghosts
  Banana Ghosts, 82
  Cookie Spooks, 85
  Dinner Ghosts, 19
  Gauze Ghosts, 29
  Ghost Cupcakes, 87
  Ghost Invitations, 65
  Ghostly Graveyard, 28
  Ghost Pops, 79
  Ghost Prints, 9
  Ghost Town, 17
  Ghost Wind Socks, 19
  Grab the Ghost (game), 73
  Recycled Ghosts, 13
  Ring-Around-a-Ghostie, 20
Ghoulish Masquerade, 29
Graveyards
  Ghostly Graveyard, 28
  Haunted Graham Cracker
    House, 88
  Witch's House Cake, 93

H

Halloween Twister, 73
Haunt Cuisine, 86

Haunted houses
  getting ready for party, 65
  Ghost Town, 17
  Haunted Graham Cracker
    House, 88
  Sign-in Mural, 64
  Witch's House Cake, 93
Headless Butler costume, 42

J

Jack-o'-Lanterns. *See* Pumpkins

L

Lawn decorations. *See also* Porch
  decorations
  Ring-Around-a-Ghostie, 20
  Trash Bag Tarantula, 22
  Vampire Strikes Back, 16
  Wicked Witch of the
    Midwest, 21
  Witch Crash, 13
LEGO-Lover costume, 54
Lunch, Halloween. *See also* Party
  food, Quick snacks,
  Sweet Treats
  Tomato Soup with Goop, 78

M

Mermaid, Littlest, costume, 51
Milk jugs
  Gauze Ghosts, 29
  Mr. Bottle Bones, 15
  Monster Jugheads, 10
Mr. Bones costume, 37
Mr. Bottle Bones (craft), 15
Mr. Postman costume, 57
Mommy Weirdest costume, 38
Monsters. *See also* Frankenstein
  Big Dipper (food), 80
  Monster Jugheads (craft), 10
  Monster Operation, 69
  Monster Paws (favor), 86
  Zombie Tag, 71
Motorcycle Rider costume, 50
Movie Stars costume, 49
Mummies
  Mummy Mug (face paint), 37
  Mummy Wrap (activity), 65

O

Old lady and baby costume, 38

P

Painting
  Dinner Ghosts, 19
  Ghost Prints, 9

FamilyFun Tricks and Treats

Ghoulish Masquerade, 29
Paint a Pumpkin, 25
Sign-in Mural, 64
Wicked Webs, 24
Pancakes, jack-o'-lantern, 81
Party favors
  Freaky Hair, 74
  Monster Paws, 86
  Slime Factory, 67
  Spider Pops, 74
Party food. *See also* Quick
    snacks, Sweet treats
  Bat Wings, 82
  Big Dipper, 80
  Haunt Cuisine, 86
  menu, 64
  Putrid Punch, 86
  Scary Face Pizzas, 82
  Skeleton Crude-itay, 78
  Snake Sandwich, 83
  Tomato Soup with Goop, 78
  Wiggly Jiggly Crystal Ball, 92
  Witch's House Cake, 93
  Worms on a Bun, 86
Party planning, 63, 65
  invitations, 65
  tips, 63
PB & Jack-o'-Lantern, 87
Pig costume, 35
Pizza
  Piece of Pizza costume, 45
  Scary Face Pizzas (food), 82
Porch decorations
  Ghost Wind Socks, 19
  Mr. Bottle Bones, 15
Princess, Fairy, costume, 52
Pumpkins
  Bubble-blowing Ballplayer, 24
  Creative Designs, 31
  Ghoulish Masquerade, 29
  Jack-o'-Lanterns, 31
  Meet Mr. Pumpkinhead, 26
  Paint a Pumpkin, 25
  Parade of Pumpkins (craft), 8
  Pumpkin Bread, 84
  Pumpkin Candleholders, 19
  Pumpkin-carving Safety, 31
  Pumpkin Patch Muffins, 84
  Pumpkin Seeds, 85
  Say Boo!, 22
  Smashing Pumpkin costume, 61
  Unidentified Flying
      Pumpkin, 25
  Wicked Witch of the
      Midwest, 21
Putrid Punch, 86

Q

Quick crafts
  Clothespin Bats, 8
  Ghost Prints, 9
  Pipe Cleaner Spiders, 8
  Recycled Ghosts, 13
  Turnip the Lights, 24

Quick snacks. *See also* Party food,
    Sweet treats
  Creepy Peepers, 80
  Edible Eyeballs, 84
  Pumpkin Seeds, 85
  Skeleton Crude-itay, 78
  Spider Pretzels, 79

R

Recipes. *See* Party food, Quick
    snacks, Sweet treats
Recycled Ghosts, 13
Ring-Around-a-Ghostie, 20
Roly-Poly Skunk costume, 35

S

Sandwiches
  PB & Jack-o'-Lantern, 87
  Snake Sandwich, 83
  Worms on a Bun, 86
Say Boo! (pumpkins), 22
Scarecrows
  Costume, 59
  Harvest Handstanders, 11
  Mr. Pumpkinhead, 26
  The Story of Scarecrows, 26
Scary Face Pizzas, 82
Sheep costume, 35
Sign-in Mural, 64
Skeletons
  Mr. Bones costume, 37
  Mr. Bottle Bones (craft), 15
  Scores of Skeletons, 15
  Skeleton Crude-itay, 78
Skin, Melting (effect), 37
Skunk, Roly-Poly, costume, 35
Slime Factory, 67
Snacks. See Quick snacks
Snakes
  Snake Cake, 91
  Snake Sandwich, 83
Soccer Star costume, 42
Special effects (costumes), 37
Spiders and spiderwebs
  Bug Attack face paint, 47
  Doorway Spiderweb, 66
  Pipe Cleaner Spiders, 8
  Spider Cupcakes, 87
  Spider Pops, 74
  Spider Pretzels, 79
  Spider Relay Race, 74
  Spider Salad, 81
  Trash Bag Tarantula, 22
  Wicked Webs (art), 24
Sports
  Boxers costume, 42
  Bubble-blowing Ballplayer, 24
  Salty Fisherman costume, 49
  Soccer Star costume, 42
Squash
  Dinner Ghosts, 19
Squirrel costume, 35
Sweet treats. *See also* Quick
    snacks, Party food

Banana Ghosts, 82
Candy Corn Balls, 88
Carrot Cookies, 91
Cookie Spooks, 85
Creepy Cupcakes, 87
Frozen Witches, 92
Ghosts Pops, 79
Haunted Graham Cracker
    House, 88
Snake Cake, 91
Spider Pops, 74
Spider Salad, 81
Taffy Pull, 79
Witch's House Cake, 93

T

Table toppers
  Apple Gals, 11
  Dinner Ghosts, 19
  Gauze Ghosts, 29
  Ghost Town, 17
  Ghostly Graveyard, 28
  Jet-black Cats, 9
  Monster Jugheads, 10
  Parade of Pumpkins, 8
  Pumpkin Candleholders, 19
Taffy Pull, 79
Tomato Soup with Goop, 78
Trash bags
  Motorcycle Rider costume, 50
  Trash Bag Tarantula, 22
  Vampire Strikes Back, 16
Tricks, Halloween
  Frankenfinger, 69
  Monster Operation, 69
Turnip the Lights, 24

U

Unidentified Flying Pumpkin, 25

V

Vampire Strikes Back, 16
Vegetables
  Big Dipper, 80
  Scary Face Pizzas, 82
  Skeleton Crude-itay, 78

W

Wicked Webs (art), 24
Wiggly Jiggly Crystal Ball, 92
Wind Socks, Ghost, 19
Witches
  Frozen Witches, 92
  Wicked Witch (costume), 60
  Wicked Witch of the
      Midwest (decoration), 21
  Witch Crash, 13
  Witches' Brew, 75
  Witch's House Cake, 93
  Witch's Stew, 73
Worms on a Bun, 86

Z

Zombie Tag, 71

Witch Crash, page 13

PHOTOGRAPHERS

Robert Benson: 9 (right)
10, 18, 50, 62, 68, 70,
71, 80 (bottom), 86
(left), 92 (left)

Michael Carroll: 4, 14, 42
(left), 64, 67 (top), 74
(right), 75, 78, 79 (top
and bottom), 83, 89, 92
(right)

Jim Gipe: 30, 31
(bottom)

Tom Hopkins: 6, 12, 16,
20, 23, 27, 95

Ed Judice: Front cover, 3,
5, 7, 8 (2 top), 9 (left),
13, 17, 21, 24, 25 (top),
28, 29 (bottom), 31
(top), 32, 33, 34, 35, 36,
37, 38, 39, 40, 41, 42 (2
top right), 43, 44, 45, 46,
47, 48, 49, 51, 52, 53,
54, 55, 56–57, 58, 59,
60, 61, 63, 65 (top), 66,
67 (bottom), 72, 73 (bot-
tom), 74 (left top), 77, 80
(top), 85 (2 bottom), 86
(right), 87 (bottom), 88,
91, 96, back cover

Lightworks Photographic:
8 (bottom), 11 (bottom),
29 (top), 69, 94 (top)

Joanne Schmaltz: 81
(top), 82 (top)

**Shaffer/Smith
Photography:** 19 (left),
22, 25 (bottom), 76, 82
(bottom), 84, 85 (top),
90, 93, 94 (bottom)

ILLUSTRATORS

Sandy Littell: 15
Donna Ruff: 26

Frankenstein, page 47

Also from FamilyFun magazine

FamilyFun Magazine: A creative guide to all the great things families can do together, from crafts and cooking projects to learning activities and travel destinations. Call 800-289-4849 for a subscription.

FamilyFun.com: Visit us at www.familyfun.com and search for hundreds of Halloween ideas, from costumes to spooky crafts to ghoulish games and recipes. There, you can also order our books from our *FamilyFun* book series.

FamilyFun's Crafts: A spiral-bound step-by-step guide to more than 500 of the best crafts and activities to do with your kids (Disney Editions, $24.95).

FamilyFun's Cookbook: A spiral-bound collection of more than 500 irresistible recipes for you and your kids, from healthy snacks to birthday cakes to dinners everyone in the family can enjoy (Disney Editions, $24.95).

FamilyFun's Parties: A complete party planner, spiral-bound, with more than 100 celebrations for birthdays, holidays, and every day (Disney Editions, $24.95).

FamilyFun's Cookies for Christmas: A batch of 50 merry recipes for creative holiday treats. In hardcover (Disney Editions, $9.95).

FamilyFun's Games on the Go: A roundup of 250 great games and tips for families traveling by car, plane, or train. In paperback (Disney Editions, $9.95).